The Eagle Soars

By the same author:-

The Jack of Clubs
The Tattered Eagle

The Eagle Soars

Geoffrey Rex Collis

The Pentland Press Limited
Edinburgh • Cambridge • Durham • USA

© Geoffrey Rex Collis 1998

First published in 1998 by
The Pentland Press Ltd.
1 Hutton Close
South Church
Bishop Auckland
Durham

British Library Cataloguing in Publication Data.
A Catalogue record for this book is available
from the British Library.

ISBN 1 85821 584 6

Typeset by CBS, Felixstowe, Suffolk
Printed and bound by Antony Rowe Ltd., Chippenham

I wish to acknowledge one-time colleagues in
273 Squadron whose reminiscences
have been of great help.

Four of those are still living:

Geoff (Slash) Adams
Ralph Ambrose
George (Lofty) Clover
and
Larry Gwinnel.

Chapter 1

From the decks of the *Orcades*, as she nosed quietly into the docks at Colombo, as dawn was breaking at the end of February 1942, the island of Ceylon seemed filled with mystique and promise. Promises of what? I wondered.

I, and the few hundred 'Singapore Harriers', as we who had been lucky enough to keep one step ahead of the Japanese advance were nicknamed, had been herded aboard the SS *Orcades* in Batavia just five short days before.

Perhaps the Good Lord was still on our side. Certainly, it was an Act of God that generated the most violent of tropical storms that had prevented Japanese dive bombers from pounding the peacetime liner of the P&O line as she eased nervously out of harbour into the Java Sea. I can still recall the chilling words of the captain as lightning struck the masthead and the sea all around: 'Anyone caught smoking on deck will be shot.' It was not quite enough to persuade me to forsake the weed – that took another thirty-five years – for smoking seemed preferable to biting one's nails; or so I thought at the time.

Now the tension of being spotted from the shores of Sumatra and as we steamed at full speed through the Sundra Straits, was a thing of the past. So too the anxious days zigzagging, unescorted by warships, across the Indian Ocean, which no doubt concealed enemy submarines.

After twelve weeks of being on the receiving end of enemy action, since the fateful morning of 7 December 1941, I reckon we all felt we were entitled to relax for a while.

To the east the sun was beginning to peep above the mountains some fifty miles inland from Colombo, its red orb reminding us poignantly of the markings on the fuselages of the Japanese Zero fighters that we had come to fear so much.

Just to the north of the rising sun I could make out, etched against a purple skyline, the unmistakeable dunce's cap shape of Adam's Peak. I remembered learning at school that Adam's Peak stood some 7,300 feet above sea level. I made up my mind that, given the chance, I would scale its summit: a holy place in the eyes of Eastern religions.

The motley legion who shuffled ashore, and on to the waiting army lorries, bore no resemblance to disciplined British Service personnel. We were more like refugees; which is really what we were.

Ceylon had been a British colony for some 140 years and prior to that, for a similar period, Dutch. They had wrested the island, in the seventeenth century, from the earliest European colonists, the Portuguese, the first to settle in the wake of the great explorer Vasco da Gama.

The Dutch had built canals and forts at strategic coastal prominences, as well as putting many local ladies in the family way to the extent of founding a Eurasian sub-race known as the Burghers. These were well respected by the islanders, considering themselves a cut above the Sinhalese and Tamils who comprised more than ninety per cent of the island's population. The Tamils had migrated from southern India, over the centuries, and were looked upon as the lowest of the social scale in the island of Lanka, as it was known by its inhabitants.

The British had developed trade, particularly the export of tea, and built military barracks. It was to the largest of these in Colombo that we were being transported, through streets bustling with rickshaws and bullock carts and pavements stained with betel nut juice expectorated by sarong-draped natives.

The Echelon Barracks might have been transported straight from Aldershot at the turn of the century, and comprised dismally long buildings around three sides of a parade ground. There we sat in groups throughout the day. Periodically, orderlies would read out lists of names, and men would troop off for some strange destination or other. I cannot recall getting anything to eat or drink as the sun arched its way across the square, but as dusk descended around the 150 or so still remaining, we were told to form up in threes and were marched towards the main Colombo railway station. Rumour had it we were set to go to China Bay, next to the large naval harbour of Trincomalee on the north-east of the island, more than a hundred miles away.

Trains had always fascinated me, and my introduction to Ceylon Railways was an experience I was looking forward to. I could still recall the cigarette cards I had collected as a boy entitled 'Railways of the World'. One of them related to Ceylon, depicting a train curving round a ledge of a mountain. It was entitled 'Surprise Point', and it captured my youthful imagination, never ever expecting I would see it for myself. My chances were not too good even now, as it was already dark before the rake of old and dirty carriages began their journey in a northerly direction, hauled by two venerable tank engines.

The prospects of getting much sleep that night were somewhat daunting. The grimy floors were covered with congealed betel nut juice, and the hard wooden seats seemed barely out of jumping range of the hundreds of cockroaches swarming around.

I decided that the end of coach lavatory door was not performing much of a service in the all male company, so I eased it off its hinges and laid it across the tops of two seat benches. It was no worse a bed than the stone floors of the King Edward's School in Batavia where I had spent five days, and was at least out of range of cockroaches.

None of us had any possessions other than the dirty clothes we stood up in and perhaps a side-pack containing a few personal belongings. But exhaustion overcame discomfort and somehow I dropped off to sleep, only to be awakened by the cacophonous protests of the two little engines as they strained every gasket to reach the top of a bank, sparks spraying out into the night sky like fireworks on Bank Holiday night displays in peace-time England. Happy memories.

It became evident that the summit of the bank was beyond the capabilities of the little engines, fuelled as they were only with wood. Coal was not mined in Ceylon, and imports had ceased with the advent of war. With a final hissing of steam we ground to a halt. Then we began to run backwards down the gradient in order to have another go at the bank. With the regulators open wide and engineers shovelling in wood blocks like dervishes the two 'Thomas' tank engines tried again, only to expire again with a gasp of steam, short of the summit.

This time the drivers broke all rules by driving the train hard in reverse to carry up the slope we had just gone down originally in order to get a better run. I was beginning to think we all ought to get out and push, as the sparks began to fly again for a third time; but this time it finally reached the summit with a sigh of steam.

A short distance up the line, as the first light of day reached out towards us, the train came to a halt, at a junction where the branch line to Batticaloa curved away to the right. There were water tanks here and we were able to stretch our legs after a long uncomfortable night while the two engines slaked their thirsts.

From there it was all downhill from the central hills to the coast, and within the hour we could see, across to the right, the grassed airfield of China Bay. On the right hand side of the field I could just make out stretches of water. On the left was China Bay itself, part of the large Trincomalee harbour. On the right there was an inlet from the open sea.

We were told we would be joining number 273 Squadron, which at dawn on the first day of March 1942 did not seem very active. In fact, nothing was moving around the few forlorn looking bi-planes scattered around the field. How could I know then that I would spend the rest of the war with the same squadron and that, in time, we would be flying Spitfires and playing our part in the final defeat of the Japanese?

On the far side of the airfield could be seen pre-war brick-built billets, with two floors above the ground floor, and other buildings a hundred or more feet further up the hill. Below the billets, at sea level, were two large hangars. Everything had been built to last, to protect the Empire and the naval base in this part of the world. It all looked so neat and tidy, a far cry from what we had been used to, particularly over the past three months. Little did we know that within three short weeks the pristine condition of RAF China Bay would be rudely shattered.

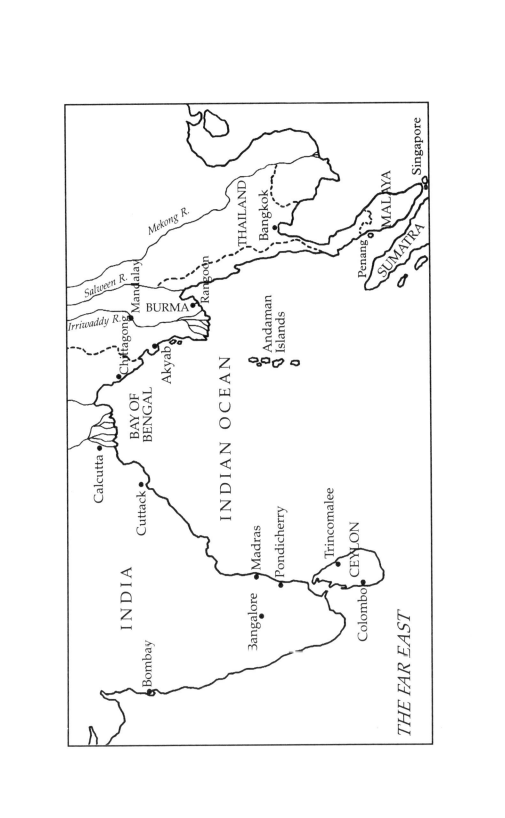

INDIA

Bombay

Bangalore

Madras

Pondicherry

Cuttack

Calcutta

BAY OF
BENGAL

Chittagong

Akyab

Irriwaddy R.

BURMA

Mandalay

Salween R.

Rangoon

Mekong R.

THAILAND

Bangkok

INDIAN OCEAN

Andaman
Islands

Trincomalee

CEYLON

Colombo

Penang

MALAYA

SUMATRA

Singapore

THE FAR EAST

Chapter 2

The Thorneycroft lorries from the RAF MT section conveyed us in relays the short distance from China Bay station to the guardroom. The little tank engines, doubtless relieved by the departure of most of their passengers, chugged off happily down the last couple of miles to the terminus at Trincomalee.

What a motley shower we 'Harriers' must have appeared to the duty NCO at the guardroom. Dirty shorts and shirts, unshaven faces, worn-out scruffy shoes and stockings; and that was the better dressed! Some, who had been plucked naked from the Java Sea after jumping from a sinking vessel, wore only a pair of overalls.

The first priority was food, as we had not eaten properly since leaving the *Orcades*. Then to the billet rooms to which we had been allocated, to find a bed space and enjoy a shower. We recognised the fact that we had rejoined the civilised world because we were issued mosquito nets, and a bed to drape them around. The beds were made by the locals who called them charpoys. In that part of the world everything in the way of furniture emanates from coconut trees, and charpoys were quite simply a stout frame supported on four-inch square legs. String, woven from coconut hemp, was threaded across the frame. Above, suspended from the ceiling beams, was the ubiquitous mosquito net.

With a blanket spread over the string this type of bed, referred to by the common airmen as 'pits' or 'wankers', was really quite comfortable. At least, they were when they were new, before the bugs moved in. Holes were drilled all the way round the frame, through which the string was threaded, giving just enough space for a malicious little bug to squeeze in and lie doggo throughout the day. At night there was a nice juicy airman to provide nourishment. By morning only numerous red swellings bore evidence of the bug's feast. The perpetrators had scuttled back into their string holes, replete and sleepy no doubt, at the first stirrings of a recalcitrant airman.

So the bug was a bugger, so to speak. Frontal physical attack by pin or wire was impracticable; there were just too many bugs. One sure way to clear them out was the injection of petrol. The main snag of this treatment was the obnoxious fumes generated. They permeated the atmosphere for quite a time, and of course created a fire hazard, for nearly everyone smoked in those days. Strange that I have not heard of any of my old mates dying of lung cancer.

The uses of petrol in the RAF, apart of course from providing the means of propelling an aircraft, were multifarious. In fact, it is a wonder there was enough left for the flying machines. Apart from its anti-bug properties it was used for any sort of cleaning, from aircraft undercarriages to greasy utensils and oily shoes. Brem, my old mate through thick and thin in Malaya and the East Indies, found another use for petrol to carry out one of his 'cunning schemes', which I will describe later.

What one misses in peacetime is the companionship of men, all around your own age, all sharing the same lifestyle and the dangers that may be lurking around the corner. Some you like instinctively, some you would prefer not to knock around with. Some were loud, some were quiet in speech and manner. I fell into this latter category; so too did Brem, with whom I had shared many happy times and many worrying times since stepping off SS *Duchess of York* in Singapore harbour in May 1941 to join 27 Squadron. His soft Caithness accent, and educated speech, even including the obligatory F word, I found to be soothing. To many a flight sergeant he was a red rag to a bull. He never did get promoted beyond Leading Aircraftsman to the dizzy heights of Corporal.

There were some who were clearly leaders of men, even if they did not aspire to NCO rank. They were usually critical of anything to do with the Royal Air Force. One such was Ginger Lacey. Ginger (I never did get to know his Christian name) was a regular airman of mid or late twenties, who had joined the Air Force before the war when jobs were scarce in the Midlands. His leonine features, flaming auburn hair and rasping voice set him apart from the others, and many enjoyed his acerbic wit and comments about life in general. He was a magnet for younger airmen, some of whom looked upon him almost with reverence.

His 'Pancho' at that time was a slightly built lad from Chesterfield always known as Slash. The nickname owed nothing to urination, as I had thought, but was in fact derived from Haile Selassie, the deposed Emperor of Ethopia, whom he resembled somewhat. Slash had good reason to be grateful for

Ginger's worldly wisdom when serving in 'X' Party at the time of the Japanese landing on Singapore Island. I never did find out what 'X' Party were supposed to do, but whatever it was they managed to get away from the beleaguered island.

Ginger was a great inventor of nicknames, quite apart from Slash. He would never use a real name if a nickname could be devised. Sometimes it was immediate and sometimes it took months before a tag became generally accepted. I always felt dispirited that I came to be known only as Ken. I did not however wish to encourage the use of 'Stinker' which some had applied, mainly on the hearsay that I had been acclaimed farting champion of 27 Squadron, probably generated by the fact that I would eat anything.

In our billet there were two Johnsons and two Smiths. The former were known as 'Geordie' and 'Gentleman'. Geordie hailed, of course, from Tyneside, and had been studying, when war broke out, to qualify as a civil engineer when the call of duty came. As such he was persuaded to help oversee the construction of a concrete runway to take multi-engined bombers. It was a very hot and dusty job cracking the whip over coolie labourers shifting earth around in baskets. Probably the conditions had something to do with the fact that he developed tuberculosis. This was only discovered when he reported for a medical examination in order to become a pilot. By the end of the year he was dead.

Gentleman Johnson acquired his nickname because of his fastidiousness. His trade in the Air Force was Fitter 2E: not the cleanest of jobs. It was said that he could change a set of plugs and then come out from behind an engine cowling still in a pristine state. The nickname 'Gentleman' was something of a misnomer, for in some ways he was very effeminate. One night he returned from the showers with his genitalia tucked out of sight between his legs. His cavorting around the billet mimicking Betty Grable was soon terminated by a swift boot up the behind.

One of the Smiths was 'Geordie' as well. His stories of sexual conquests would take too long to relate here. There must have been lots of libidinous ladies in Sunderland.

Rommel Smith was quite a different character. Rommel was supposed to resemble the newly appointed chief of the Afrika Korps; but there the resemblance ended. He hailed from Highbury, in North London, and was one of a family of eighteen whose father played the drums in an orchestra. Because of this he developed a passion for classical music, and later managed to scrounge a collection of records in order to give evening recitals in the mess. He had little sense of humour, and was perhaps rather boring, but was the right sort of bloke to have around in a tight corner.

Later on there was posted to the squadron a third Smith. At eighteen he was the baby of the flights, but he had the most strident voice, as well as suffering from verbal diarrhoea. Ginger immediately christened him 'Tannoy' which did not deter him from hanging around his idol, to an extent, I feel sure, that Ginger found embarrassing.

Enough of nicknames. There were many more that will crop up from time to time. Suffice to say that all these assorted types, thrown together by the chance of war, would in time cement together to form the backbone of a greatly inflated 273 Squadron.

The business end of the squadron, the aeroplanes, hardly warranted that description. Because of China Bay's proximity to the naval base of Trincomalee the planes were sea orientated. Half a dozen Wildebeests, capable of carrying torpedoes; one Walrus, a flying boat with a single pusher engine; and a Seal. All dated back well before the war, and were bi-planes. Excepting the Walrus, they were encased with fabric covering wood and metal frames. There were Wildebeest squadrons in Singapore which were annihilated within days of the outbreak of war. With top speeds around 100 m.p.h., downhill, they were like clay pigeon shooting for the Japanese Navy's Zeros.

The Seal was the oldest plane of the lot, harking back to the 1920s, and was more of a joke than anything else. I only saw it airborne once, but somehow it survived the raids in April, and probably lives on in a museum somewhere in the world.

All in all, early in March 1942, 273 Squadron could be considered something of a Cinderella outfit. But later in the month reinforcements were flown out from the naval base in Alexandria in the shape of Fairey Fulmars. These were handsome planes with retractable wings for use on aircraft carriers, and with an extra seat behind the pilot for a navigator or observer. Again, their top speed, on account of their heavy construction, nowhere near matched the Hurricane, which itself was slower than the Jap Zeros which could be expected to pay a visit before too long.

In the meantime, on this first day of March, the sudden influx of manpower to the squadron was something of an embarrassment. On arrival we were hungry and dirty, with no change of clothing, and many needed medical attention.

The cookhouse coped well with the first of our needs. The camp's water supply was soon being taxed to the full; and then we sampled the luxury of our own charpoys, lying starkers while our meagre clothing dried in the sun.

Gradually, throughout the month, our kit was replenished by supplies flown down from stores in India, and service life once more resumed a more orderly pattern, as we had had in Malaya before the Japanese invasion. We, the ground crews, were divided between flights A and B, but because of the excess number of technicians there were rather more than three airframe and three engine fitters to carry out duties on each kite. Therefore there was plenty of leisure time.

In peacetime this part of the island was considered a favourite place for holidays. The planters up in the hills would enjoy the sea, with its many sandy beaches and languid palm trees. China Bay was not a favourite place for most Service personnel because there was no town nearby and thereby no female company to pursue.

Within the camp boundaries there was access to a swimming area in the sea, fenced off to discourage sharks. In fact, I heard nothing about sharks in those parts, so I only used the facilities once, preferring the beaches and the open sea. On that one occasion some of the lads were happily splashing around in the altogether when they were surprised by an officer's wife making her way down the rock path for a swim. In peacetime, officers were allowed to take their wives to suitable postings abroad. This lady was awaiting a berth on a ship to be repatriated, as Ceylon was now reckoned to be in an active war zone. Perhaps someone had told her that the sea was swarming with naked men.

The next day, I and two or three others, made our way along a jungle path seaward to a beach some two miles from the camp. The warm blue water and little sandy cove took my mind back nostalgically just a few weeks to the blissful two days spent with Tau Fong on 'Love Island' in the Java Sea whilst awaiting repairs to the *Hang Tau*. In my mind I could feel the smooth silky curves of her lissom body as she lay on the silver sand. Tears welled up in my eyes. I knew I must face up to the fact that I should never see her again, but my memories would never let her die.

Later in the week I was off duty at the same time as a West Country fellow whose name was Paddon, but on whom Ginger Lacey had bestowed the nickname Herman the German, on account of his tall blond Aryan frame. Herman, who was true blue and patriotic, did not like the tag in the least, but was too quiet and gentle to raise any fuss.

We decided to go down to the nearest bay, where there were a few fishermen's dwellings, to see if we could hire a catamaran. All the native canoes had parallel outriggers secured to the hulls with a couple of branches of trees. The handing over of a few cents soon secured use of a canoe for a few hours, so away we paddled out into the harbour of Trincomalee, Herman at the back and me by the crossrigger in front.

All went well for about an hour, by which time we were far out into the second largest natural deep water harbour in the world when, without warning, the prow of the canoe suddenly plunged straight into the water and I was left floundering in the briny. The fact was that Herman's twelve stone weight was rather too much for the frail craft, and he had been sinking steadily lower in the water, but without breathing a word to me up front. Once relieved of his weight the canoe immediately nosedived, and headed for Davy Jones' locker.

In spite of having been ship wrecked before, I did not consider myself to be a strong swimmer. The nearest shore looked an awfully long way away, and there was nothing to hang on to. After what seemed an age the wooden craft returned sluggishly to the surface, as if it did not relish the prospect of being boarded again by two heavy Englishmen. The local fishermen were small wiry types. We could not board it as it was upside down, and the outrigger rendered it impossible to roll over in the water. There was nothing for it but to swim with our legs, pushing the catamaran before us towards the shore from whence we had embarked.

After swimming for longer than I had ever swum before, we could make out, in the far distance, another canoe being paddled rapidly towards us. Rescue at last, we thought, as the craft drew near, with two fishermen aboard. Wrong. Their thoughts were only of salvage, and we were left to soldier on by ourselves. The couple of hundred yards or so seemed more like miles in our near state of exhaustion. On the shore we dropped our shorts to dry in the sun and spread out our worldly wealth, in the form of dollar notes, to dry on the hot rocks. A tree stood near the shore that was inviting to climb. Maybe, I thought, I would be able to see from up there the nearest way back to camp.

Only once before had I climbed a tree in the nude, and that was because Tau Fong was already up there, in a similar state of undress, gathering coconuts.

The incentive was not the same this time, but erotic thoughts came flooding back that stirred my memories, and my loins; but tears were again not far away.

On the 25th of the month number 261 Squadron's Hurricanes touched down at China Bay. Their ground crews had already been installed in the billets a few days earlier. We knew that another Hurricane squadron, number 30, was ensconced at Ratamalana, the pre-war civilian airport seven miles south of Colombo, and also that 11 Squadron's Blenheims had taken over the old racecourse in Colombo. Army units also were beginning to take up positions around the camp and harbour. Indeed, things were beginning to warm up. If Japan had military designs towards Ceylon it was likely to happen soon. Could we, would we, be ready to ward off the enemy?

Chapter 3

By the end of March 1942 there were forebodings that once again we would be closely involved with the war. Whatever planes could be spared from India, or off carriers, were being flown in to China Bay and the Colombo area. More Fulmars arrived for us to look after, and a couple of flights of Swordfish for the naval boys.

On 24 March, Darwin, in northern Australia, had been bombed. The Japanese strike force that had annihilated the US fleet at Pearl Harbour on the fateful dawn of 7 December 1941 had returned to the fray as Singapore fell to their army, and had carried out mopping up what was left of Allied shipping in the Far East at the Battle of the Java Sea. The very formidable and highly honed forces of Admiral Nagumo, still virtually unscathed, would now be refuelled and recharged for their next foray. Would it be southwards, to colonise Australia? – the Darwin raid seemed to indicate that it might be – or would they move westwards towards India and Ceylon? The Andaman Islands, roughly down the middle of the Bay of Bengal, had already been occupied by the Japs.

These were the topics of discussion one evening as we waited to be entertained by a military band of a Kentish regiment who had set up their chairs and music stands in the quadrangle surrounded by the billets. The lights came on and darkness descended as the band struck up. I can't remember much about the band's performance, only that of a pariah dog bonking away vigorously on top of a bitch on heat, with another bitch on standby. They moved slowly, with only six paws on the ground, into the floodlighting that had been temporarily rigged up. I wonder if the band ever knew why their rendering of the William Tell overture was causing such hilarity. For an encore the dog, panting furiously, set about the other bitch, finishing by getting himself dog-knotted, and not being able to move for quite a while. Nevertheless, his tongue was still hanging out in evident satisfaction!

Had we but known it, as we watched the dog and band show, the Japanese fleet was indeed heading our way, with orders from the Japanese High Command to 'seek out and destroy British sea power in the Indian Ocean'.

The newly appointed Admiral Somerville, in command of the Eastern Fleet, knew full well that Nagumo's far superior forces would probably be moving westwards. In Ceylon all seaworthy shipping was ordered to scatter from the two main harbours, Colombo and Trincomalee. The naval ships were to assemble at a hastily prepared base at the southernmost tip of the Maldive Islands. We watched as the camouflaged warships, both great and small, including the aircraft carrier *Hermes*, steamed purposefully out of Trincomalee harbour. Our thoughts then were that when the Japanese air forces came our way the lack of shipping in the harbour would lead them to pay greater attention to the air base. How right we were proved to be.

In the nick of time, as it turned out, a small contingent of Catalinas, the US twin-engined flying boats, had flown halfway across the globe to base themselves in a lagoon named Koggala, near the southernmost point of Ceylon. The Catalina's great range of nearly thirty hours' flying time rendered them far superior to any other craft in the task of searching for the enemy who were sure to observe radio silence, as they had done on their approach to Pearl Harbour, in order to maintain the surprise element of attack.

At dawn on 4 April, as the patrolling Catalina, under the command of Sqn/Ldr. Birchall, was some 350 miles south-south-east of Ceylon and about to turn for home, the crew spotted a small speck on the extreme southerly horizon. They turned south at 200 feet to investigate. As they closed in for identification it was seen that the lone vessel was just one in advance of a huge fleet of battleships, carriers, destroyers and supply ships.

Birchall must have known as he veered north at full speed, barely half the capability of the Navy Zeros, that his chances of reaching the base were virtually nil. As the wireless operator hastily started transmitting his information to base the first flight of Zeros was already airborne, intent on destroying the Catalina. The Zeros were with 20 mm cannon firing small explosive shells which ripped into the doomed Cat, just as a repeat of the message was completed. The transmitter was destroyed and two of the seven-man crew were injured before the plane force landed on the sea.

Admiral Somerville was informed immediately, and calculations were made which predicated that the Japanese air attack would probably be launched on

Colombo the following morning – Easter Sunday.

Before dawn the fitters of 30 Squadron were warming up their Merlins ready for the pilots to take off at first light. Six Fulmars of the Fleet Air Arm were already on patrol down the east coast in mainly cloudy conditions. The Hurricanes of 258 Squadron, stationed on the Colombo racecourse, were also at the ready.

From China Bay at dawn the Swordfish of the FAA 788 Squadron, armed with torpedoes, took off for Colombo in two flights of three. If they were to encounter the Japanese armada steaming north it would seem to be a suicide mission.

At a quarter past seven, in the old Dutch fort at Galle, a huge air armada was sighted out at sea heading north. In spite of all the apparent alertness at Ratmalana the Hurricanes of 30 Squadron were caught on the ground when dive bombers appeared overhead. At the racecourse, six miles to the north, 258 Squadron had a few precious minutes notice to get airborne. It did seem that the vital information transmitted to base by the doomed Catalina's crew the previous day was being squandered.

Soon the dive bombers, believed by many to be the same that had wreaked havoc at Pearl Harbour four short months before, were screaming down on ships in the harbour. Indeed, there was little enough in the way of shipping as most warships had been ordered to scatter when it was known the Japanese force was on its way.

By coincidence, and with great misfortune, the six 'stringbags', as the Swordfish was known, that had left China Bay earlier with torpedoes to attack the Japanese fleet, were forming up in line to land at Ratmalana for refuelling. Within minutes all six had been downed by Zeros that peeled off from the canopy of fighters protecting the bombers. Most of the Swordfish crews were killed.

On the credit side, the Hurricanes of 258 Squadron had clearly not been detected by the Japanese taking off from the racecourse strip, probably because they were not aware of its existence. Most of the casualties suffered by the Japanese Air Force on Easter Sunday were inflicted by the Mark 2B Hurricanes of 258 Squadron.

Of 30 Squadron's planes, only seven remained serviceable after the Japs had returned to their carriers for refuelling. Had they then resumed the offensive the squadrons would have been heavily outnumbered. Of the fourteen

Hurricanes airborne from the racecourse only five returned to base. Most of their pilots had been killed or were in hospital. In all, including the Swordfish, twenty-seven planes had been lost in the Colombo raid. However, it was claimed that a like number of Japanese planes had also been downed.

It came to be known later that a second wave of bombers, intended to follow up the first attack, had been diverted to deal with two of our Navy's destroyers, the *Dorsetshire* and the *Cornwall* which had been sighted steaming south by a Jap reconnaissance plane. Both ships were dive-bombed and sunk.

Our planes at China Bay were too far away to give support to the defenders of the raid on Colombo on Easter Sunday, but we knew that our turn was likely to come soon, probably within the next few days. Admiral Nagumo, not having been able to engage the British Eastern Fleet, must surely have thought their ships would be in Trincomalee harbour. Admiral Somerville, however, mindful of the fact that his fleet was inferior by far to that of the Japanese, had been able to effect a withdrawal, undetected by the enemy, to the southern extremity of the Maldive Islands, south-west of Ceylon. It would have been suicidal of the British fleet to have engaged the enemy in daylight, and the opportunity of a night attack never arose.

Blissfully unaware of naval manoeuvres, but nevertheless apprehensive of imminent attack, we lowly airmen had rifles thrust in our hands at dawn on Easter Monday and were marched to an open space on the airfield perimeter. Fortunately for me there were not enough rifles to go round on a permanent basis so I had to borrow one for the sake of the exercise: I never had aspired to marksmanship.

In groups of three we had to charge over the grass, with fixed bayonets, towards three sacks hanging forlornly from a goalpost. 'Them's not just sacks of straw,' yelled the Army Warrant Officer, 'make 'em bleed and scream.' It quite put me off my breakfast.

It was the same thing on the Tuesday, and the Wednesday. Still there was no attack. Perhaps the Japs weren't going to bother. Wishful thinking.

On the Thursday morning I was due to report at the sick bay to have sores on my legs treated. Most of the 'Harriers' had fallen victim to some disease or other. I was one who had developed dermatitis, which was very uncomfortable. I had therefore arranged for a colleague Fitter 2A to see my Fulmar, piloted by Flying Officer Gregg, off on dawn patrol.

I had just climbed the hill behind the billets to the sick bay when I was aware

16

of 261's Hurricanes taking off, and the air became filled with noise and tension.

For a few minutes the roar of engines subsided as the Hurricanes disappeared across the harbour at full boost to gain maximum height. Four of 273's Fulmars were also airborne, including F/O Gregg on my plane which 'Pasty' Morrell, a quiet Cornish lad, had seen off for me.

Within a few short minutes other noises, the menacing screech of hostile planes diving, shattered the air. Instantly I forgot all about my dermatitis treatment and dashed outside the building from where there was a commanding view across the airfield. I was just in time, for one second, to look down on a Navy Zero, its pilot clearly visible at a distance of no more than a hundred yards as he flew between me and the hangar roofs, cannons blazing. The rising sun emblem behind the cockpit canopy struck fear into my heart. I took off for the boundary fence as fast as my sore-riddled legs would let me. As I did so there was one great explosion behind me.

Slash, who was too close for his own comfort at the time, told us afterwards that it was our precious petrol bowser that had been hit. He was near enough to be spattered with blood from the bowser's tractor driver, whose body below the waist disappeared in the explosion.

Aftermath of the Japanese Task Force raid on China Bay airfield. April 1942.

Slash and Ginger were cowering in a shallow ditch when there was another shattering explosion as ammunition laboriously stacked the previous week between the hangars by our men, in spite of their protests about the vulnerability of the site, shot skywards. I was just about to clear the boundary fence at that moment, so it greatly assisted my lift-off. Athletically, I had never been one for the high jump, except of course, metaphorically! Normally I would have picked my way through the strands of barbed wire, which now I had cleared in one bound!

On landing I glanced over my shoulder to see the underbelly of a Zero as the pilot jerked the stick back to clear the hill ahead of me. Soon I was amongst the stunted trees that covered the steep rocky side of the hill. It seemed like safety at last as I clambered upwards. I was on my own except for the gibbons I could hear chattering in the trees away to my right. Doubtless they were as frightened as I was about the strange cacophony that was shattering their calm. The monkeys were not aggressive, but they were mischievous. They had pulled off the cockpit covers and odd protruding bits of the aircraft that we had sweated only the day before to clear out of the hangars and disperse among the trees. It proved to have been a wise move to disperse the Fulmars awaiting servicing and repairs in the hangars, for within minutes bombs were raining down on China Bay. Somehow it had not occurred to me that we would be subjected to high level bombing as well as to dive bombers and fighters. But there they were, as I peered through the foliage from my rocky prominence, wheeling around at about ten thousand feet, apparently unopposed by our fighters which were considerably outnumbered, and being kept very busy by the Zeros.

I could see smoke rising from the shattered hangars, with their metal roofs a tangled mess. The officers' mess also had been hit, and in between were our billets with most of the tiles missing.

The bombers wheeled around for perhaps ten minutes that seemed like ten hours. No doubt they found themselves short of targets as nearly all the shipping, indeed anything afloat that was seaworthy, had previously been ordered out of the harbour when Admiral Somerville considered an airborne attack was imminent.

The SS *Sagaing*, from which we erks from A and B flights had been unloading crates over several days, had been beached close to the airfield perimeter and was now well ablaze. The ammunition painstakingly removed from the *Sagaing* was the very stuff that had headed towards the heavens minutes before.

Strangely, only a small amount actually exploded, and raw gelignite from out of the bombs and machine gun ammunition was scattered around the hangar apron almost ankle deep. More about that later.

In the meantime the drone of bombers had receded, and the Zeros presumably had needed to return to their carriers to refuel. A lone Hurricane came in to land, its engine coughing and spluttering, with smoke trailing behind as its belly tore across the grass in a cloud of dust. Later we learned it was piloted by Flt/Lt. Fulford of 261 Squadron, who during his flight had shot down at least two enemy aircraft. Subsequently, he was awarded the DFC.

Another Hurricane was damaged beyond repair on landing, but the pilot escaped. However, two of his colleagues went down with their planes, and four others were injured.

I made my way down again from my rocky hide-out to see what help I could give, and to see my plane back to its dispersal point, giving as wide a berth as possible to the smouldering hangars and the carnage that surrounded the shattered bowser.

At the 273 dispersal hut there was much disarray and gloom. Three of our four Fulmars that were airborne limped back home, but still there was no sign of my plane, with F/O Gregg piloting. As minutes stretched into hours we knew he would not be returning. Indeed, his plane and body were discovered eventually in a swamp down south near Batticoloa, where they had lain undetected, except by scavenging beasts, for nearly two years.

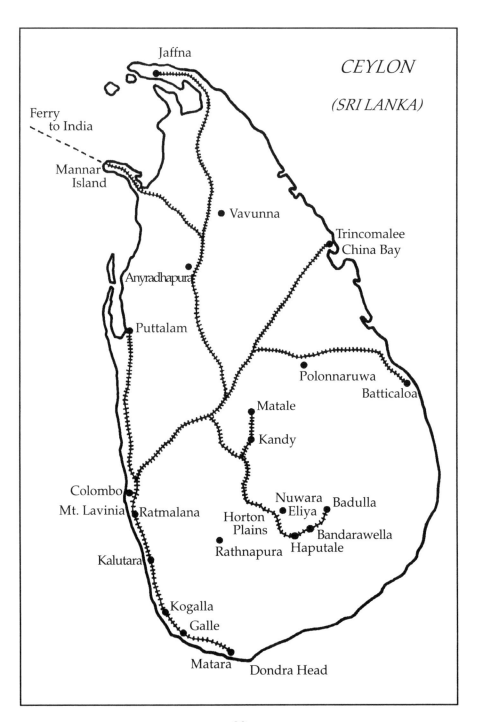

CEYLON

(SRI LANKA)

Jaffna

Ferry
to India

Mannar
Island

Vavunna

Trincomalee
China Bay

Anyradhapura

Puttalam

Polonnaruwa

Batticaloa

Matale

Kandy

Colombo

Mt. Lavinia   Ratmalana

Nuwara
Eliya   Badulla

Horton
Plains

Bandarawella

Kalutara

Rathnapura   Haputale

Kogalla

Galle

Matara   Dondra Head

20

Chapter 4

For the rest of that fateful day, 9 April, we waited expectantly, having hastily prepared for standby what planes could still be made serviceable. It was pitiful compared with the obvious strength of the enemy. We did not know then that we were probably saved by the aircraft carrier *Hermes*, but to her cost.

The *Hermes*, with no serviceable aircraft aboard, as all the Swordfish and Fulmars had been used in the defence of Ceylon, had left Trincomalee on receipt of Admiral Somerville's instructions to scatter. It was her misfortune that, when only some hundred miles south of Trincomalee, she had been spotted, whilst the raid on China Bay was actually taking place, by a Japanese reconnaissance sea plane.

The Captain, aware that the enemy bombers were sure to be called into action, turned around to try to return to harbour, or at least to lie as close to the shore as possible.

Admiral Nagumo, unaware that the *Hermes* posed no threat, ordered his reserve planes, that were being held back in readiness for a follow-up raid to Trincomalee, to attack the carrier.

The *Hermes* captain, with no air cover from his ship and unaware that the RAF at China Bay were otherwise engaged, radioed Colombo for help. He was well out of range of the Hurricanes, but bravely, 11 Squadron's eleven serviceable Blenheims took off to cross the central mountains of Ceylon, rising to 8,300 feet, and then to fly out to sea beyond the east coast. Two of the planes had to return with engine trouble, but the remaining nine pressed on gamely, choosing the Japanese flagship, the *Akagi*, for their target. Bombs straddled the target, regrettably without effect, as the Zeros pounced on the luckless Blenheims. Only four planes, all of them damaged, limped back to the racecourse in Colombo.

In the meantime, the *Hermes*, after suffering withering attacks from dive bombers in her attempt to reach harbour, finally sank some five miles off-shore near Batticaloa. Many who had survived the bombing and had swum clear of the carrier as she sank were picked up later by a small British ship, whilst seven made it by swimming to the shore.

Back on shore, we waited for the expected troop invasion. We were not to know then that there was no troop carrier; the armada was purely a carrier task force, with attendant naval craft and supply vessels: indeed, the same strike force that had wreaked such havoc at Pearl Harbour just four long months before. Unbeknown to us the armada, having been unsuccessful in seeking and destroying the British Eastern Fleet, was by now returning to refuel in the Andaman and Nicobar Islands. For Ceylon the danger was over; but we erks were not aware of that.

At dusk we crept back to our billets, fearful that we would be called to arms before the night was out. Across the bay a large oil storage tank was on fire, sending a great pall of black smoke high into the sky. That, we thought, would act as a marker for the enemy to home in by. In fact, the oil tank burnt for four whole days; but still the enemy did not come. Some said that the Japanese plane that had ignited the oil tank had had its tail shot off by a Hurricane, but others had said that they had seen a Zero circling round before diving straight into the tank. We did not know anything then about kamikaze pilots.

Between the billets and the shattered hangars we could see the flicker of a small fire. Someone said that it had been lit on the instructions of the Station Warrant Officer to cremate the three who had been killed on the ground. The next morning we found that it was all too gruesomely true. The fire had not done its job very well.

That night, the lads on the second floor, without a roof over their heads, moved down to wherever they could find room on our floor. Actually they need not have bothered as the monsoon was not due for some weeks.

The next morning the tension had lifted a little as we picked our way through the rubble to 273 Squadron dispersal hut. Compared with 261 Squadron, who had several Hurricanes to repair, our Fulmars had suffered very little. Of the four that managed to get airborne, three had returned unscathed, and the fourth was simply missing. The Fulmars that had been dispersed in the jungle were wheeled back on to the airfield during the morning and got ready for take-off. But again the call to scramble never came.

No sooner had the echoes of the bombs died away than the rats began to leave the sinking ship. Or rather, the local populace began to stream out of Trincomalee and nearby villages. Our room boy was one of the first to disappear. He was a nice lad, with handsome features and wavy black hair. He had served the men in our billet faithfully since we had moved in, for just a few cents per person per week. No doubt he had heard through the grapevine, or whatever was the Tamil equivalent, that the Japanese were not very nice people. Their soldiers would rape the womenfolk, and shoot anyone without mercy. Better to get away inland to the jungle where they could hide. So the dusty road we could see across the airfield was covered by a straggling line of colourful sarongs shuffling westwards, laden with all that they could carry. When the train to Colombo pulled out of China Bay station there was little room left on the carriage roofs, and the buffers were well occupied too.

The effect of this evacuation on the Service personnel stretched beyond having to make up our own beds, and do our own dhobying (washing). It also affected our rations. No longer did we get any fresh meat or poultry, however tough it may have been; it was back to bully beef, and a curious sort of sausage made out of soya beans. I was one of the few who could stomach it.

There seemed to be nothing we could do about the prospects of an unending boring diet. Nothing, that was, for all except Brem. He came up with one of his cunning schemes. He was never put off by the fact that his schemes usually ended in disaster. This one proved to be no exception.

Over the days immediately after the raid the ammunition that had been scattered by a well directed bomb was still lying ankle deep between the ruined hangars, and men were beginning to gather up the smaller particles of high explosives. These were little black chips, rather like the seeds of leeks. Some men made crude fireworks with these, while one slightly mad electrician, nicknamed Scouse for obvious reasons, sprinkled some on to the concrete billet floor, arranged in the shape of a hammer and sickle. A lighted match tossed into the middle, a sudden whoosh of flame and for ever more the Soviet emblem was etched into the flooring. I never knew whether Scouse was a member of the Communist Party, or whether his action was meant to denote solidarity with Uncle Joe Stalin, who was then our ally – nominally, at least.

Brem had a more practical idea in mind, intended to help supplement our diet. I should have known better than to let him involve me in his scheme. I daresay it was because I had something of a reputation for being able to scrounge odd things. After all, I had been able to make a suitcase out of a cockpit cover stretched over a spruce frame strengthened with odd bits of duralumin, all fixed together with screws milked from the billet's light fittings, embellished with leather straps relieved from a 15 cwt truck. The *pièce de résistance* was a lock borrowed off a store cupboard. The main snag was that the finished article was almost too heavy to lift, and that was before putting anything in it! Nevertheless, my handiwork followed me around for the rest of my service days, ending up gathering dust in my loft in Palmers Green.

Returning to Brem: his immediate needs were a Coca Cola bottle, a long length of flex, a Fulmar starter cartridge and a six-volt battery. I am sure he did not use such things in his youth when fishing off the coast of Caithness. Here in China Bay it seemed to him quite an appropriate method of gathering a quantity of fish in a short time. The bottle was easy, and was soon filled with the chips of cordite. Scouse, the mad electrician, soon came up with several yards of flex. It was not difficult to purloin a Fulmar starting cartridge; this I did whilst carrying out the morning's DI (daily inspection). By tiffin break Brem had connected the flex to the starter cartridge, sealing it into the bottle with a handful of gunge and winding the flex around the bottle. The battery was a little more difficult, requiring the co-operation of a MT driver. Smokey, the Cockney from Shoreditch, was not difficult to bribe with the promise of a fish, but we would have to meet him later at the MT section when the sergeant wasn't around. That fitted in well with Brem's plans to carry out his instant fishing expedition by moonlight. In the meantime, we decided to hide the bomb in a locker on the top floor, which was empty since Jappo had lifted the roof off.

All went well with Smokey, who had already planned to cut up spuds for chips, and Brem and I took it in turns to carry the battery to a quiet cove near to where Slash was caught with his trousers down, well out of sight of the main camp. The sun was just touching the horizon as we hid the battery behind a rock and headed back to the billets for tea. Feeling rather pleased with ourselves, and savouring in our minds the thoughts of a midnight fish feast, we were met by Geordie Smith as we approached the billets.

'If I were you, lads,' said Geordie, with obvious relish at being the harbinger of bad news, 'I would keep out of the way until after lights-out time.'

'What the f— for?' exclaimed Brem, frowning.

'Bloody Red Caps have been round searching the billets and found your bomb,' said Geordie. 'They think they may be on to a saboteur, so they've been

24

quizzing everyone in the billet. Of course, nobody knew anything about it, but the Red Caps might just remember you two weren't there. On the other hand, they are probably too stupid.'

'Fish and chips are off for tonight,' I said to Brem, 'and we had better be too.' We hastily turned and began to retrace our steps.

'And any other night too,' responded Brem. 'The bastards are sure to have taken away the evidence, and we can hardly ask for it back, so we might as well return Smokey's battery before his sergeant notices it is missing.'

As we watched the lights go out we crept quietly back to our room and into our beds. Nothing more was said during the days that followed, so the Red Caps must have decided that the mystery of the Coca Cola bomb was beyond their sleuthing capabilities.

As the month of April wore on we all began to breathe more freely, for it seemed that an enemy landing in the manner of those in Malaya, Sumatra, Java and numerous smaller islands was becoming increasingly unlikely. We knew that had the Japanese landed on the east coast of Ceylon, the island would probably have been theirs within days. The RAF could have effected little more than a token resistance to a seaborne invasion anywhere along the many miles of beaches. The two Hurricane squadrons on the island, numbers 30 and 261, were barely at half strength, whilst 11 Squadron's Blenheims had been rendered harmless.

The British Army was too thin on the ground, with just a few Indian regiments and the Ceylon Light Infantry, consisting of a few planter officers in charge of raw recruits. The capture of Ceylon would have opened the back door to the sub-continent. India had long been restless under British imperialism and could easily have become the rotten apple that would have allowed the link-up east and west with the German forces that were not too far away in the Caucasus and North Africa.

It was little wonder that the raids on Ceylon, which had been hailed by the Allies as proof that the Japanese could be repelled, had caused concern to Churchill. When lecturing in America after the war Churchill was asked what, in his opinion, had been the moment to cause him the most anxiety during the whole of the Second World War. Probably to the surprise of his audience he had cited the news that a Japanese task force had been sighted approaching Ceylon.

On the ground at China Bay we slowly began to shape our Cinderella

25

squadron into something approaching a fighting force, or as near as we could get to it whilst equipped with Fairey Fulmars. A few more planes turned up after the raids, and now we had enough for two flights of six to be kept serviceable.

Occasionally mishaps occurred: like the time when I nearly retracted an undercarriage whilst carrying out a DI. The engine fitter and a kindly airframe sergeant who happened to be nearby, held up the starboard wing until I could hastily get more help to lock the undercart again. The sergeant did not report the incident, so I was saved a spell of jankers, or worse.

Another incident that I recall involved an armourer who, when cleaning a Browning gun in one of the wings, fired off a couple of rounds that somehow had been left in the breech. His foot was hanging over the leading edge of the wing at the time, and the bullets scored a hole in one of his shoes, but without puncturing his foot. There was much swearing from the cooks across the airfield as the two rounds seared through the cookhouse wall at about head height. Fortunately, the two cooks, Westwood and Whitham, were bending over their pots at that moment or it might have affected our catering arrangements!

I had been in the Air Force nearly two years, and this was the first opportunity I had actually to fly. I think the pilots quite liked a bit of company during a test flight, and for us it relieved the monotony of just sitting under the wing whilst on stand-by.

Chapter 5

Around the time of the raids we had a new Commanding Officer posted to the squadron by the name of Sqdn/Ldr. Constantine, known by all, behind his back at least, as Connie. Connie was not a man to bother about what erks called bullshit; but he was able to command respect, and without raising his voice. He was a natural flier, having survived the Battle of Britain, and led his pilots in the air by example. However, he had his weaknesses, one of which was drink. Quite often he would appear at dispersal, having been on a bender in the mess, and commandeer the nearest available aircraft. He reckoned there was nothing like a few aerobatics to clear a thick head. We hardly dared look as he took off straight across wind, and the normal landing strip, then straight up over the billets with not many feet to spare. Somehow he always came back to land safely.

Such antics only served to endear him to all of the men, and a generally good spirit pervaded throughout 273 Squadron. The constant threat of invasion, during the weeks after the raids, helped in the cementing of camaraderie.

It was as well that an *esprit de corps* pervaded for there was little to do in leisure time but talk and drink whenever there was beer in the NAAFI. There was no town to visit, no cinema and, more important, no women to be chatted up. There was football about once a week between the various sections, and, later on, cricket. The orderly room clerk, Corporal Bell, who was a cricket enthusiast, produced from somewhere enough equipment, and a strip of matting to stretch over one corner of the airfield when no flying was taking place.

Later on, a camera club was formed by two or three enthusiasts, which was how I became hooked on a lifelong hobby.

It was soon after the raids that Brem had another of his ideas. This one could be described as spontaneous combustion rather than a cunning scheme. We had not experienced anthills before coming to China Bay. They seem to be more common in hot dry climates where the soil is porous, and can often rise to several feet above ground level. One such mound was within our dispersal area, not very far from the flight hut. The countless termites that beavered away building their home must have been doing just that for many years, but did not really bother us. Other creepy crawlies, such as scorpions that would often hide beneath wheel chocks, were of much more concern.

Perhaps Brem had received a nip from a termite and that gave him the idea to teach them a lesson. Being Brem, he did not broadcast his method of retaliation which involved pouring half a can of petrol down the termites' main entrance, then running the fuel in a line to a point a few yards away where he quickly struck a match and lit the fuse line to cause a flame. In fact, he must have created just the right mixture of fuel and air, akin to the cylinder of an internal combustion engine, to cause an explosion – and quite a big one at that.

The muffled boom, and small clods of earth spattering on Fulmar wings and the dispersal hut, rapidly ejected Flight Sergeant Fulford from within. Chiefy Fulford was a dapper little man with a waxed moustache and a very florid countenance. On this occasion it had turned bright puce, and the waxed moustache was twitching.

'What the f— hell was that?' exploded the worthy Flt/Sgt.

'It was only Brem, Flight, demolishing an anthill,' volunteered Lofty, the airframe corporal, trying to be helpful, and taking the opportunity of a spot of crawling.

'I'll give him f— ant hills,' ejaculated Chiefy, perhaps relieved that it wasn't another Jap raid, and no apparent damage had been done. He didn't like termites any more than he did Brem, with his educated tone of voice; but as the culprit had already beaten a hasty retreat the matter was allowed to rest.

About this time in the month of May, mail from Blighty, that had been held up since before the start of hostilities in the Far East, began to trickle in, but not necessarily in chronological order. Some was a good six months old.

It was a great relief to know that my parents were still unscathed in the autumn of 1941, but they must have been very worried in December when I, like the other Harriers, was reported missing. For our part we were worried by recent reports of heavy night raids by the Luftwaffe on London, Coventry and other cathedral cities and ports. It was then that I learnt that my brother had married a WAAF. Perhaps I would be an uncle by the time I reached home again. The lack of comment from my mother about the nuptials led me to believe that she disapproved of the match. This surmise proved to be correct.

To my surprise, amongst my old mail was one from my girl friend from whom I had parted the day before boarding the SS *Warwick Castle* in Glasgow to set sail for the Far East. On that last night, before boarding a troop train in Wilmslow bound I knew not where, I had written to her saying that I did not expect her to wait for me as I would be away for at least four years, which seemed a lifetime then. Our relationship was not serious; certainly I had no thoughts of marriage in 1941. Whilst gazing later across the Atlantic and Pacific Oceans I did come to regret having written that letter. Anyhow, I did not expect she would still be available in 1945 when my spell of duty overseas was due to end.

In the meantime, during those desperate days in Penang after the Japanese invasion, I had met Tau Fong and fallen in love. Her delicate charm had beguiled me, and she returned my love to the full as we tried to keep one step ahead of the enemy. As she disappeared in the terrible bomb explosion that wrecked the *Hang Tau* in the Palembang river a part of me went too.

Time was beginning to heal a broken heart, and this letter from Doris did something towards mending an aching void. The letter was not couched in loving terms, but at least she was concerned about my wellbeing. Indeed, when she wrote I had been reported missing, and therefore her efforts might well have been all in vain.

After three months of unremitting sun, a state that would doubtless have been envied in England, the skies began to cloud over and soon the monsoon from across the Bay of Bengal was upon us. It was welcome to enjoy a shower of rainwater as it cascaded off the roofs.

Within a week or so the sun was once again more in evidence, and the threat of rain began to subside. So too did the threat of invasion, and we began to relax more. At the time we were unaware that the seemingly invincible Japanese fleet had suffered setbacks in the naval battle of the Coral Sea. Although the US had suffered also, their industrial and financial reserves were far superior to those of Japan. Many of the pilots and their aircraft who had pounded Ceylon, just two months before, were lost in the Coral Sea.

With the relaxation of stand-by duties it became possible for the 'flights' to allow crews to enjoy some leave, the first that I had been able to take since leaving England fifteen months previously. I paired up with another fitter who could be spared for a seven-day break, whose accredited nickname was Whisky.

Not surprisingly with the surname Hague.

We knew of no other place to spend our freedom than Diyatalawa, the rest camp in the hills where some of those who had been ill had been sent to recuperate. For me it meant the thrill of a long train journey across the mountains.

This time the second class compartments were rather more comfortable than the cockroach-infested cattle trucks in which we had made our first journey by Ceylon Railways.

Three quarters of the way back to Colombo we alighted at the junction of Polagahawela where the up-country line headed towards the hills. This was when I was soon going to experience 'Surprise Corner', the view from a mountain ledge, with a train snaking round it, that had so captured my imagination on a cigarette card in my youth. As is so often the case, anticipation can often lead to disappointment, and the views across the plains from the carriage window did not exactly meet up with expectations. At a mere 1,600 feet above sea level it was no great deal; but from Kandy Junction, not far along the line, the magnificent engineering skills of our Victorian forefathers became more apparent as the line made its tortuous way southwards through the mountains. Many tunnels and bridges gave glimpses of great waterfalls as the double-headed train snorted its way up to the summit, over Horton Plains, at a height of 6,226 feet, before earning its rest, freewheeling down through Banderawella, and on to the halt at Diyatalawa.

The rest camp had sprung up almost overnight with the great influx of troops into Ceylon earlier in the year, many of whom were stricken with sickness. The cool, clean air at the altitude around 4,000 feet was no doubt of great benefit to those convalescing, but for Whisky and me, who considered ourselves reasonably fit, things became rather boring after a couple of days, in spite of the camp having a cinema, which was something we had not experienced for many months. After three nights sharing a hut crowded with a rather motley mob of servicemen I managed to persuade Whisky that it would be a great achievement to scale Adam's Peak.

The next day we boarded the Colombo bound train back over the summit to Maskeliya, the nearest station to Adam's Peak, and booked in at a bed and breakfast establishment. I cannot remember much about the place except for the fact that it had a bath. It must have been fifteen months since last I had submerged myself in warm water; showers, to me, were no real substitute, and the pleasure of wallowing in a tub was something I did not realise I had missed so much.

An early start next morning for the twenty mile trudge to the peak made us realise we were not so fit as we thought we were; and this was the easy way to scale Adam's Peak! Later I was to scale the holy summit by a more difficult route.

Initially, the path wound through tea plantations. This was my first close contact with the origins of what supplied our early morning cuppa and was the staple refresher for millions. The small bushes, rather like unruly privets in suburbia, were a bit of a surprise. Dotted amongst the bushes, with large wicker baskets like those we would use to put the dirty linen in tied to their backs, were a small army of dusky women. The dexterity with which they cast every handful of green leaves over their shoulders was quite therapeutic for the passer by, but doubtless was gruelling and boring work just to earn a chapatti at the end of the day.

The 'dunce's cap' of Adam's Peak was probably little more than a couple of thousand feet above the plain when approached from the east, but was quite enough for our tired limbs at the end of a twenty mile trek. On the pinnacle was a temple-like structure which sprang to life only on days holy to those whose religions take them on pilgrimages to this place of worship. Those who are especially devout, and athletic, would make the ascent from the west, an arduous six thousand feet up from the plain. I made up my mind I would try it, if possible next New Year's eve. Looking down from the top, the prospect was somewhat daunting.

On this June day the summit was deserted and we could not spare much time to admire the truly magnificent view before wending our way back to catch the train.

In spite of a whole week spent with Whisky we did not strike a close friendship although we got on well enough with one another. But wartime service was often like that: men came and men went; posted in and posted out. Some left their mark in one's mind, but only the odd one or two did I keep in contact with in post-war times. I cannot remember what happened to Whisky.

By the end of June the monsoon was just a memory and the unbroken, boringly unremitting sunshine was with us again. In truth, I was beginning to miss the excitements that had gone before. There were no more bombs to dodge, no women to seek out, and nowhere to go within walking distance.

About this time we were told that our boredom would soon be relieved, in the shape of a move to a new airstrip to the south of Colombo, called Katukurunda. The squadron would move in two sections, the main body, including me, to go first to get things ready to receive the Fulmars, whilst a skeleton crew remained to clear up after seeing the planes off. The move was to be made by road, and I was to be one of those detailed to travel on the 'Queen Mary', which was the RAF nickname for a sixty-foot articulated recovery vehicle usually used if a plane pranged away from the airfield.

I was pleased to be making use of the suitcase I had constructed, even if it took two of us to lift it when full. A new adventure was underway as the driver skilfully manoeuvred the lengthy Queen Mary out of the gates of China Bay.

Chapter 6

Once again I was in and out of Colombo without being able to look around as our ungainly vehicle made its way into the north-east suburbs, and straight out again due south down the coastal road towards the old Dutch fortress of Galle, passing by Mount Lavinia and Ratmalana, which were to become familiar to us later on.

The airstrip at Katukurunda, twenty-three miles south of Colombo, had been constructed hastily by clearing a swathe of rubber trees, leaving just about enough room for a single runway, with the aircraft dispersed on either side. Indeed, there was not much margin for error when landing and taxiing a Fulmar. This fact was soon to be demonstrated by a certain sergeant pilot who landed too heavily on one wheel and bounced off a couple of parked planes before coming to a halt in a cloud of dust.

In peacetime it would have been quite an idyllic spot, particularly as we were billeted in a castle some three or four miles from the airstrip.

Richmond Castle, which was supposed to resemble its English counterpart, had been constructed at the turn of the century by a local chieftain who had amassed a fortune from rubber and tea. It stood on a prominence some 200 feet above the Kalu Ganga river and was constructed of brick and plaster stucco, fashioned to resemble limestone, which was a commodity not readily available on the island. The main gates leading to the house (castle seemed too grand a description), had been damaged by transport belonging to a contingent of Australian servicemen who had just vacated the place. The unkempt lawn in front of the house was adorned by little plaster statues and ornaments, also slightly the worse for wear.

I was one of the first to enter the house, mainly because I was suffering from a mild attack of dysentery at the time and there was only one place I needed, and in a hurry. I dashed up the bare wooden stairs hastily seeking out the smallest room; and there in the gloom, to my great relief, in more ways than one, stood a wooden commode. As an airman once commented, it is the second most satisfying physical function to evacuate oneself under pressure. Unfortunately, I had not had time to inspect the furniture beforehand, and the fact that there was no bucket beneath the seat turned out to be quite a serious omission!

There was almost a holiday atmosphere about the time spent at Katukurunda. It was the first time in my service life that I had been billeted outside a fenced area. To reach the airstrip, or indeed anywhere away from our sleeping quarters, it was necessary to use motor transport. The ubiquitous three-tonner Thorneycroft, with its high tailboard and canvas roof, usually provided our mobile needs; but there was the odd 'toastrack' bus, which must have been commandeered from the Colombo Bus Company, and gave quite a novel ride to and from work. It had quite a surprising turn of speed, and was quite happy ploughing through about a foot of water when the Kalu Ganga river overflowed its banks following heavy storms in the mountains.

Looking down on the swirling brown waters of the river as it flowed past our castle prominence, I could not help thinking once again of the Palembang River in Sumatra, as the love of my life had been swept downstream in the tangled wreckage of the *Hang Tau.*

It was here in Richmond Castle that I became close to two good friends with whom I kept up contact in later life. They were both engine fitters, and both hailed from the West Country; Pedlar was a Bristol man, living as a teenager in the suburb of Fishponds, whilst Mo was a true son of the soil from the ancient town of Glastonbury, in Somerset. Both had their nicknames bestowed by Ginger Lacey. Pedlar was the more orthodox one, with the surname of Palmer. It was good alliteration, and no doubt stemmed from the ancient journeymen who plied their trade on foot in medieval times.

The name Mo was much more original. It came about one beer night when most had become paralytic and had staggered into their mozzy nets in a stupor. Mo was a large angular man with a strong stomach and a large bladder capable of accumulating quite a number of pints of beer. He kept going after everyone else was horizontal, and in his deep fruity Somerset voice was giving a stentorian rendering of a popular tune of the thirties entitled 'Old Mona'. He had just got as far as 'Old Mo' when he stumbled base over apex down the stairs on his way to the loo. The name 'Old Mo' stuck for ever more, and somehow seemed singularly appropriate.

Katukurunda was a pleasant enough place to be stationed, with a castle for living quarters, but like China Bay there was nowhere nearby to provide entertainment for the off-duty airman. If there was a village of Katukurunda I never found it. The nearest town was Kalutara, but that had little to offer Europeans. Galle, down the coast towards the southernmost point of Ceylon, Dondra Head, was certainly European in origin, but of a bygone age. The old castellated fort, with its cannons facing seawards, might have been a deterrent to raiders in centuries past but would not be a lot of use against the Japanese. After all, big guns facing out to sea had not deterred the Japs on Singapore Island!

There was little else to do in off-duty hours except drink beer. Connie, the CO, was all for a tipple, particularly if it kept the troops happy, and did his best to obtain supplies direct from the docks in Colombo. On one occasion he persuaded some local planters to invite the whole squadron to their club. With free drinks all round it does not require much imagination to visualise the state of many airmen, including the CO, when the appointed hour arrived for the return to the billets. Many were laid out paralytic on the lawn outside the club's pavilion, and had to be thrown into the RAF transport.

Had the squadron stayed much longer at Katukurunda it is likely most would

One of the first Hurricanes to arrive. On standby. October 1942.

have ended up alcoholics; but after a couple of months living in Richmond Castle rumours were afoot that we would be moving up the road to Ratmalana, the pre-war airport for Colombo.

In fact, it had been decreed that we would be parting with our Fulmars and taking over 261 Squadron's Hurricanes. Their personnel would then move up to Burma and be re-equipped with Spitfires. Around the end of August we were moving north again, this time a mere fifteen miles to the airfield that had also suffered at the hands of the Japs some four months previously.

Our pilots ferried the Fulmars up to India for the use of the Fleet Air Arm, returning by train and boat to take over the Hurricanes. I think we were all glad, and proud, to be working with these tried and trusted aircraft that had accounted for themselves so well in the Battle of Britain. There was a sense of pride in becoming a real fighter squadron, with planes that could give as good as they could take, even with the dreaded Zeros.

Within days of moving to Ratmalana came the third anniversary of the outbreak of the Second World War. At the time it seemed we were no nearer winning it, and indeed, no end was in sight. If the Eighth Army failed to hold Rommel's advance in North Africa to capture the Suez Canal then the war might still be lost, in spite of the potential power of the USA. In Russia, the battle of Stalingrad was at a critical stage, and could go either way. If all went wrong we were still in a vulnerable situation in Ceylon. If the tide did turn our way, then our squadron could be brought into action in Burma before too long. Also, perhaps we had discounted the importance of the American Navy's victory over the Japanese Navy at Midway Island. Maybe we had become too overcome by continuous defeats and propaganda, to believe that there had been a victory.

In the meantime, for us menial erks it was a question of making hay whilst the sun shone. No longer did we have a castle in which to sleep or, indeed, the brick barracks of China Bay. Here at Ratmalana we were billeted in the stereotype atap huts constructed entirely of the ubiquitous coconut palm. The long trunks provided the main supports, whilst the leaves were cleverly plaited to serve as walls and roofs, which surprisingly let in very little water, in spite of the very heavy storms that hit us from time to time. The whole wooden frame was secured into concrete bases of sufficient size to accommodate a couple of dozen airmen. In fact, two huts conveniently housed the ground personnel of both A and B flights. The huts were shaded by palm trees and other assorted flora, some of which, such as plantains and mangoes, provided welcome additions to our diet. From the A flight hut it was perhaps two hundred yards uphill to the cookhouse, and about the same distance downhill to a gap in the fence that was close to the flight dispersal hut situated on the north side of the airfield. There was no concrete runway at Ratmalana in 1942. Our Hurricanes, on practice scrambles, would take off up the slope in groups, line abreast.

To the north of our billet was a kind of back entrance to the camp, maintaining a guard hut, leading to a lane which led to freedom.

Just outside the camp entrance was a Singhalese café called the Bernice, where passable European food could be consumed. The long lane wound its way down for about a mile to the main coast road, past pleasant bungalows mostly owned by middle class Singhalese or Burghers. Just a short walk beyond the busy coastal road, where buses to Colombo were frequent, was the renowned beach of Mount Lavinia. On a headland prominence to the south of the beach was, and still is, the Mount Lavinia Hotel, then strictly for officers only.

It was here that I learnt to surf ride. There were none of the large plastic boards of the present day, on which one can stand, but a plain plywood strip, some four feet long by one foot wide, with a curved and bent leading edge. One could only lie on them, gripping firmly by the front end. After numerous duckings the knack of jumping onto a roller at the right moment was acquired and the exhilaration of being swept into it, and conducted right up the beach, was a fulfilling achievement. After a couple of hours battling with the surf of the Indian Ocean one came out of the sea perspiring and in need of the beachside showers.

That was how many an off-duty period was spent when there was not the time to journey the seven miles into the centre of Colombo. I had had three brief encounters with Colombo without having had the chance to get to know the place. The first time was a view from the decks of the *Duchess of York* in May 1941, on the way to Singapore: the second was six months earlier when the *Orcades* docked from Java. Then it was just a day on the parade ground of the Etchelon barracks, not an experience to be repeated when off-duty, and an evening sighting of the main railway station. The third was a brief flirtation with the suburbs as the Queen Mary made its way from China Bay to Katukurunda.

Colombo was a much larger city than I had thought, boasting its own tramway system. The trams converged on the old colonial part known as the Fort, adjacent to the docks, where most of the government offices were situated.

As servicemen we were mostly interested in the Services Clubs, where English meals could be had for a few cents; also the cinemas, of which there were six or seven. I don't believe there was a red light area; or if there was I never found it. In fact, the Singhalese ladies, often very attractive in their brightly coloured saris, always seemed intent on keeping out of the way of British servicemen, probably thinking that they only had one idea in mind; and they were probably right. I expect that anything could be arranged at a price, but we did not have that sort of money. Strolling through a local street market one day with Pedlar and Mo I recall the sharp eye of the latter spotting a familiar looking little container for sale. Condoms, or french letters as they were then known, were not easy to come by, even if you didn't get the chance to use them. Mo was quite excited about his purchase, until he found the rubber had perished. No doubt it was second hand – at least!

Most of the cinemas were of the fleapit variety, although the films showing, usually American, were reasonably up to date. Flea pit was literally an apt description as from time to time they would have to close for fumigation. If the film was an absorbing one you might not notice the bugs feeding just below the line of your shorts until getting outside into the fresh air.

The move to Ratmalana provided the first chance for me, since joining the RAF more than two years previously, to present myself before a promotions board. I did not have any great ambitions in the Service, but it would be nice to have another shilling in my pocket for gaining the distinction of the rank of aircraftsman first class. It was about the time I decided that I had better take more pride in my job or else I might be posted away from 273 Squadron. Usually those who couldn't be bothered about their work were the ones to be posted away if a vacancy occurred elsewhere. That was quite understandable on the flight sergeant's part, and I had narrowly avoided being sent down to the Catalina squadron at Koggala. Luckily I had found someone keen to swop with me. I had made good friends in 273 Squadron, and also enjoyed the general atmosphere of the squadron and the attitude of the officers towards the airmen. A new pilot had just been appointed to my aircraft, F for Freddie, a young Pilot Officer named Laughton, who earned the nickname Charles on account of the well known Shakespearean actor of the thirties. I got on well with Charles, who may well have thought that his life might depend on me one day, so I, in return, was prepared to put in a little extra to ensure his plane was always in a serviceable condition. It always looked better if the fuselage and undercarriage were kept clean, which meant sweating in the sun with a petrol soaked rag. Anyhow, my newfound conscientiousness may have helped in gaining promotion.

The chance to take a further week's leave arose in the autumn of 1942. This time I teamed up with Pedlar, the Bristolian, who had been a keen cycle racer before the war, but shared with me a love of mountains.

We had both heard about Nuwara Eliya, the 'English' village, with its racecourse, more than six thousand feet up in the mountains. The place is pronounced 'New Raylier', so it took me quite a while to reconcile the sound with the spelling on the map of Ceylon. Firstly, we took the train to Kandy, the one-time capital of the island before the advent of international commodity trading resulting in the development of the port at Colombo. Kandy was still the religious centre of Ceylon, being particularly holy to Buddhists as the home of the Buddha's tooth. I never found out if the Buddha only had one tooth, but I do know that it had been encased in its shrine at Kandy for many centuries. Once every year, or on special occasions, it was paraded with much pomp around the streets of Kandy on the back of a highly adorned elephant, with many saffron-robed priests in attendance. So a visit to Kandy was a must.

The Buddist Temple of the Tooth, Kandy.

39

Everything in Kandy seemed to be holy. The lake near the temple; the fish in it; and the elephants being scrubbed down by their mahouts in the river. The lake would have been a paradise for fishermen had they been permitted to ply their skills.

The town lies in the centre of Ceylon at around 1,500 feet above sea level, in the foothills of the mountain massif. It was not as cool as we had hoped, and the clanging of holy cymbals throughout the night at regular intervals gave us little chance to sleep in our quarters next to a temple. So we only stayed one night.

By train and bus we journeyed up the next day to Nuwara Eliya, some 4,500 feet higher up, nestling in a valley below the highest mountain in Ceylon, at 8,300 feet, Mount Pedro. After the coastal plains, where temperatures hovered between 80-90° Fahrenheit, it was a good ten degrees cooler, and more like an English summer's day. The planters who had developed the tea estates all around had also turned this valley nostalgically into a little oasis like their homeland. To the south of the old village were many colonial style bungalows with views across the valley, with its lake, and the racecourse at one end. All was green, cool and peaceful.

Author aged twenty-two.

40

We booked in at a small hotel run by a middle aged English couple who had moved down from India when the husband retired from the Army. It was here I was introduced to curry as it should be prepared and served, with a line of white jacketed waiters offering small dishes of meat and spices for selection. As I did not know just what I was selecting, and did not wish to show my ignorance by enquiring, the roof of my mouth suffered excruciatingly.

From the balcony we could watch the sun setting behind Mount Pedro, the highest, if not the most spectacular, of the Ceylonese mountains, which beckoned us for the following day. Neither of us could resist the challenge of climbing the highest point just because it was there.

In fact, the ascent of two thousand odd feet from Nuwara Eliya was not arduous, and within a couple of hours we were looking down all around us. I could not help thinking how much my father would have liked to have been with me. It was he who had instilled in me the desire always to reach the highest point, wherever you may be. Now he was in his sixties and beyond the hope of conquering any more peaks. Life had been hard for him, anchored to a clerical job in the City of London, with only retirement to look forward to, and that had been put on ice until the end of the war. Both his sons, and there were no daughters, were serving in the RAF and might not even return at the end of the war; if that ever came about.

Indeed, it was at this time that the British forces had their first convincing success with the defeat of the German Afrika Korps at El Alamein. As Churchill said at the time, 'This is the beginning towards gaining victory', or words to that effect.

For us in Ceylon the prospects to the north in Burma, where sometime we could expect to be sent, seemed to be a stalemate where we were just waiting for the enemy to make the next move. True, the exploits of the Chindits gave some hope, but their endurance and bravery only served to emphasise the difficulties of the task ahead. However, we erks were just very small cogs in a vast machine, and at the moment we were in a backwater of the worldwide conflict, and so we might as well make the most of our lives.

For me, that meant playing cricket whenever possible. We could muster a fair degree of talent in the squadron, and there were quite a few teams in the Colombo area. Usually we were beaten, even by the schools, many of whose sixth formers showed great skill and dedication to the game. I thought at the time Ceylon ought to become world contenders of cricket one day, and maybe even play England in a test match at Lords.

The end of the first week in December brought the first anniversary of the war in the Far East. It had seemed a very long year since those first harrowing days, followed by the escape from the advancing Japanese army. As Christmas Day came around again I recalled the previous year in the sanctuary of the Wongs' home in Penang, with the conquering Japanese soldiers too close for comfort. Comfort for Brem, Fruity and myself came in the shapely forms of the three daughters of the absent head of the Wong household. It was Tau Fong who gave me the fulfilment of love over that Christmas time. My loins tingled at the thought; but now I must realise I could never hope to see her again; but the memories would not go away, and tears came into my eyes.

Christmas Day fell on a Friday, although it was not a holiday for those of us on the flights, as at least one section was kept on alert throughout daylight hours, seven days a week. But the cooks put themselves out to serve a Christmas dinner as near traditionally as they could, and of course, there was plenty of beer available. To generate a more homely atmosphere one hut was furnished and decorated to resemble an English pub, with a skilfully painted signboard outside depicting a racing hound, with the title 'The Whippet Inn'.

On Sunday, the squadron cricket XI played the local hospital staff. We lost convincingly in spite of my personal best bowling performance of 5 wickets for 18 runs. I countered that by being bowled for a duck.

One of the team, named Tony, expressed keenness to join us on the projected scaling of Adam's Peak by Pedlar, Mo and me to see the sun rise on New Year's Day. It needed to be accomplished within forty-eight hours because of our duties. It was an adventure which could well go wrong.

On New Year's Eve the four of us set off soon after dawn to journey the first fifty-one miles to Ratnapura, the gem mining centre in the foothills. A hitch on an army lorry and a local bus got us to the town in good time for lunch at the local planter's club. Here we negotiated the hire of a car to take us as far as it was possible to go by road towards the mountain. The car had seen better days, but somehow managed to chug its way to a small village at the end of the road where the driver had arranged for us to be met by guides.

The Sherpas were slight of frame, and not in the first flush of youth, but soon proved that they had stamina as we began the thirteen miles and six thousand feet climb to the summit. As storm clouds gathered around we had qualms about going through with the expedition, for when Tony fell lame with cramp it soon became apparent that we would not reach the summit before sundown.

We toiled resolutely on as the sun sank behind the coastal plains and it became increasingly difficult to make out the path ahead. At the halfway stage we came across a primitive hut, presumably erected for the use of pilgrims. Pedlar was the one with the most experience of mountaineering, so we looked to him as our leader.

'I think we ought to rest here for a while,' Pedlar pronounced. 'The moon should be rising in two or three hours time; it would be best to launch our final assault by its light.'

'I'll start a brew up,' volunteered Mo, always a man for a cup of tea. He was startled initially by the presence of a small snake in the corner he had selected to kindle a fire. The snake seemed more afraid of Mo than he of it. The eventual cup of char, with a Mars bar, helped to restore our spent energy, and Tony and I managed to snatch some sleep before the light of the moon made it possible to resume our trek.

Without our guides, who knew where footholds had been cut in the rock face, I doubt if we could have surmounted the more precipitous parts. At one point lengths of chain had been secured into the rock to haul oneself upwards.

To our surprise, as we approached the summit strange wailing noises penetrated the darkness. Our guides assured us that it came from pilgrims already ensconced in the little temple, and was not anything supernatural. We were told that we should remove our shoes as we approached the holy area where a depression in the rock was said by Buddhists to have been the footprint of the Buddha himself when he journeyed that way many centuries ago.

We approached slowly, holding our shoes, a little apprehensive lest we Christians might be resented by the assembled wailers, some of whom wore the saffron robes of Buddhist priests. But clearly they were peaceable people, as surely they would have been brought up to be, and we in our turn kept out of their way as they went about their incantations, fervently lowering their heads to the ground as the first light of dawn of the new year spread across the eastern sky.

At the approach of the sun on the horizon I looked down towards the way we had come. I reckoned it was as well we had climbed by moonlight as I might not have had the nerve to carry on in broad daylight.

We had already toasted in the New Year with Mo's brew of tea, but now I began to wonder what 1943 would have in store for me and those sharing my life. Undoubtedly 1942 had been the most momentous year of my short life – I would be twenty-three in a fortnight's time – and I was simply lucky to have survived so far. I had gained, and then lost, the first fulfilled love of my life. Perhaps in the year just starting the tide of war would turn, and the thousands of miles separating me and my mates from our families and loved ones could soon be breached.

Chapter 7

The New Year at Ratmalana started serenely enough, the threat of invasion now being just a memory. The two main reasons for feeling secure in Ceylon were firstly, the fact that the Eastern Fleet was still operating from South and East Africa, well out of range of any Japanese armada, apart from the odd submarine; and secondly, that the retreat of the Afrika Korps in Tunisia, in the aftermath of El Alamein, was moving apace: never would the enemy reach the banks of the Suez Canal.

For us it was a question of keeping boredom at bay until such time as the squadron might be wanted to replace one of the fighter squadrons already operating in Burma.

At the end of January we heard that just such a move was about to take place, but it was not to be 273 for the long journey north just yet. We were set to relieve the fighter squadron at China Bay who would be moving into active service.

I cannot say that the prospects of moving back to China Bay were received with any degree of enthusiasm, but we erks could do nothing about it.

Finally, after many delays, we moved by road out of Ratmalana on 15 February to replace 17 Squadron who were then on their way to Burma. One good thing was that China Bay had now been tidied up. Repairs to the barrack block roofs, damaged in the April raid, had now been carried out, and there was also a camp cinema. We found out also that rations had improved since the bully beef days of the previous year. So two of the main requirements of the ordinary airman were now on hand, entertainment and reasonable nosh: but still no crumpet, of course!

Just before moving from Ratmalana I had received confirmation of my promotion to Leading Aircraftsman. It was nice to have a few shillings more each fortnightly pay day, even if there was not the opportunity to spend it in

Trincomalee. There was kudos too in having a pair of 'props' to sew on the arms of my tunics.

Much of my spare time was now being taken up in the dark room which had been set up in a disused storeroom in our barrack block by Mo and Pedlar. The former had been employed pre-war in a chemist's shop in Glastonbury, and thereby knew all about the processing of films, as well as about french letters. Pedlar too, had embraced the hobby of photography, and between them I, and a few others, became absorbed also. It was a hobby that stood me in good stead for many years after the war, and saved many a needy pound when capturing on film the early years of the young family. Only the advent of colour slides and films in the sixties caused me to pension off my enlarger and developing chemicals in my own little dark room in the attic.

There were two anniversaries in March that I found rather depressing and which prompted me to apply for a transfer to flying duties. On the first of the month I had completed one whole year in Ceylon. Although I much appreciated the attractions of 'The Jewel in the Indian Ocean', I was becoming restless for action and the prospects of adventures in other places. Little did I know that I would see out another year still on the island.

The second anniversary was on 19 March: two years since boarding the *Warwick Castle* in Glasgow Dock, bound for overseas service. Theoretically, it marked the halfway stage of a tour of service overseas for a single airman. In practice I was expecting to be longer away from the shores of England.

At times I felt homesick, particularly as Doris was now corresponding regularly, and had advanced to three XXXs at the end of each letter. This was reciprocated, without committing myself too much.

I suppose that the thought of having the chance of renewing my friendship with Doris was one reason for my application on 17 March to re-muster as a Flight Engineer. The need for an engineer in flight had been introduced into the RAF, only since my departure from England, with the advent of the big four-engined bombers brought into active service. The control of fuel supplies and other airframe complexities had become too much of a burden for a pilot on a bombing mission, so provision was made in Lancasters and other giant bombers for an engineer to be housed in the centre of the aircraft surrounded by gauges and beneath a gun turret where the flight engineer would be expected to man a Browning gun in the event of enemy fighters attacking.

Actually, the flight engineer, seated as he was between the main spars, had the least chance of parachuting out in the split seconds only that there might be in the case of an emergency. The RAF had already lost nearly half of the original intake including my old friend Harry who had joined up with me at Uxbridge in 1940. He was lucky to survive a parachute jump over Germany, suffering no more than a broken leg, followed by three and a half years in Stalag Luft 3. That happened on his first mission! Because of the rather rapid demise of flight engineers the RAF was casting its net further afield than the UK and I was one of the bloody fools to stick my neck out. In fact, there was no certainty I would be accepted because I had already been turned down at my pre-service 'medical' for training as a pilot because of an astigmatism in my right eye which meant my capacity for focusing clearly on anything at more than eighteen inches was impaired. That would have been a distinct disadvantage when piloting a plane.

Anyhow, I thought that perhaps the eyesight requirements for a flight engineer were not so stringent as for a pilot. After all, I only needed to see a distance of about two feet to read instrument gauges, and my chances of hitting an enemy aircraft with a machine gun were virtually zero.

Very little re-training was required for an aircraft fitter, so my name was sent forward to Bomber Command headquarters in England by my CO. I sat back and waited. And waited. The months ticked by and my enquiries at the Orderly Room always drew blanks. It was sometime in the autumn before I was summoned, and then only for a medical test.

In the meantime I had become friendly, but not too friendly, with a medical orderly known as Oscar. Oscar certainly displayed homosexual characteristics, but was the kindest of individuals. I recall him relating a story about a WAAF medical orderly, which must have taken place in England, for there were certainly no women in the RAF in Ceylon in 1943. He said that she came up to him rubbing her erotic parts against his body declaring she was feeling randy. No doubt she knew he was queer, and was just taking the mickey out of poor Oscar.

Anyhow, the MO had delegated my initial eyesight test to Oscar who carefully set up his chart on its easel outside in the sunlight, and then gave me every chance to pass the test by adjusting my chair around so that it ended up a few inches nearer. My left eye, without the astigmatism, was always 100%, so this one he tested first, and I was able to memorise the vital second line from the bottom before he covered over my left eye for testing the dodgy right one. So far so good; but I told him that I had failed my test in 1940 when confronted with a darkened room with just a pinpoint of light showing on a screen. I then had to state which side of that point of light was a line projected from a machine by the MO. As I could see two lines the test was a non starter. Oscar whispered in my ear that the MO always tested in the same sequence: left, centre, right, centre and right again. I would not have got through the test without that piece of information, for after three years since my initial testing there were still two lines of light moving around in parallel.

That night, having also passed my aptitude test, it was beers all round for my mates who expected me to be sent on my aircrew course within a few weeks. Naturally, they all thought I was a bloody fool, and I was inclined to agree with them.

The examining officer told me to get in as much flying as I could by way of acclimatisation. Our squadron being equipped only with single seater Hurricanes the opportunities for flying were somewhat restricted.

One chance was the dawn patrol carried out daily by the Dutch squadron of Catalinas stationed at China Bay. They would allow me on board as an observer because our squadron was also involved in the exercise. It will be recalled that it was as a result of information radioed back to HQ from one such aircraft, early in April the previous year, that we had been forewarned of the approaching Japanese armada.

By moonlight my mate and I were ferried out one morning with the Dutch aircrew to the waiting Cat, bobbing about at its moorings in the bay. There were three such amphibious craft kept at China Bay, and every morning since the raid one set out in darkness heading towards the Andaman Islands from whence any enemy was likely to approach, be it by air or sea. The dawn patrol also provided practice for our Hurricanes, four of which, armed with cameras mounted in the wings in place of the eight Browning machine guns, would set off at first light to try to intercept the Catalina. If successful, the Dutch airmen would be called to the guns, loaded with blanks, and do their best to keep the attacking Hurricanes in their sights. We were told we would not need parachutes, only 'Mae Wests', as the plane would fly over water all the time and would put down on the sea if it got into trouble.

It was a most exhilarating experience when our Hurricanes appeared in the sky above as I positioned myself between the two gun blisters amidships. The Catalina also had a gun position available in the under-belly by raising a trap door and poking a Browning out through it, whilst the gunner suspended himself by means of a wire attached to his belt at one end and the upper fuselage above. A very large Dutchman, presumably the navigator, took up that position, making the slender wire look very inadequate. When not looking upwards through the blisters I was confronted downwards by his capacious bottom. In fact, I was too busy hanging on for dear life, as the pilot threw the lumbering Cat around the sky, to worry about falling to oblivion through the trap door. The manoeuvrability of the Catalina was really quite remarkable as the pilot spiralled ever downwards to gain the comparative safety of the wave tops where the Hurricanes could only attack from above, and the Dutchman with the belly gun and large arse became redundant.

It was all great fun as we skimmed the wave tops and 'shot up' China Bay on returning to base, landing in the bay with a touch-down noise that sounded like the hull being torn off. The four-hour flight had generated a great appetite for breakfast. As I downed my egg and bacon I could not help reflecting upon the fact that the exhilarating experience of the Catalina dawn patrol, carried out with cameras and blanks, was a far cry from being in the bowels of a Lancaster as it dodged the searchlights and flak over Hamburg. The glamour of the dawn patrol would be supplanted by the sheer terror of the night-time mission.

As 273 Squadron no longer had twin seated Fulmars there was no opportunity to fly unless something unusual occurred. This happened one day when a lone Harvard, piloted by a young Canadian, touched down for servicing. The pilot was a gung-ho extrovert who boasted that he could make anyone sick who went up with him. The Harvard, with its passenger seat, like the Fulmars, behind the pilot's position, was in need of a test flight after its servicing. So I stuck out my neck and volunteered for the vomit test; after all I knew that I did not suffer from seasickness, having only once spewed up aboard ship, and that was when anchored on a millpond sea off Bombay, and was more to do with stale kippers consumed for tea than anything else.

One difference between the Fulmar and the Harvard was that the latter was a training plane fitted with dual controls. As we climbed in the young pilot said airily, 'If you are still well enough after the aerobatics you can take over for a bit.'

This was strictly contrary to regulations, but that did not seem to bother the Canadian. So he climbed to ten thousand feet and put the plane into a dive for the first loop, followed by a succession of rolls and more loops. The trick of making a passenger, who did not know what was coming next, part with his breakfast was to alternate the rolls left and right rapidly. It very nearly worked with me, but somehow I managed to hold on to my fried egg. As the intercom had become disconnected during the aerobatics the pilot was unable to tell me what he was going to do next, so he simply held both hands above his head and I found that the joystick was responding to my pressure. I don't think I did many of the right things but at least we stayed airborne.

That was the one and only time in my life I had the chance to pilot an aircraft, and we would have been court-martialled had the authorities known about it.

The month of April 1943 kicked off with a special parade to mark the inauguration, twenty-five years before, of the Royal Air Force. As Ginger commented, 'What other day of the year would you expect the RAF to be formed than April Fools Day?'

Also during the month came news of events that marked distinct evidence that the fortunes of war were turning towards the Allies. The Germans finally surrendered in Stalingrad, and the Eighth Army entered Tunis. The surrender of all the Axis forces in North Africa could only be days away.

For me, and the same three mates who had scaled Adam's Peak on New Year's Eve, leave time had come round again. Quite naturally we gravitated to the mountains for a fourteen-day break. I would never tire of exploring the mountain region of Ceylon. Apart from the welcome drop in temperature and humidity there was always somewhere fresh to explore. This time it was the discovery of Horton Plains, a remote mountain plateau at 7,000 feet above sea level, with several small lakes that attracted fishermen to the small Rest House which was eight miles from the nearest road. It was a haven I was to visit again, more than once, during my time on the island. The solitude was reminiscent of the Yorkshire Moors, and the welcome blazing log fire in the lounge at eventide was a poignant reminder of home.

The nearest rail point to Horton Plains was a halt at Pattipola, less than a mile from the 6,226 feet summit of the line, from where it was a two hour hike to the Rest House. Not far from the station we came across a dwelling resembling an African kampong, with its round thatched roof, and smaller buildings to match. We had been told by the guest house owner in Nuwara Eliya that an eccentric, but interesting, couple had settled there.

Ignoring the sign on the wicker gate, 'not at home', we approached the odd-looking building with some trepidation, to be met by a stocky middle aged lady dressed in riding habit, with a revolver hitched to her belt.

'I'm Mrs Palliser,' she said, by way of introduction. 'Come in and meet my husband.' Tony, acting as our spokesman, introduced us, and let it be known we were on our way to Horton Plains Rest House.

Commander Palliser, RN retired, was an impressive figure of a man, probably twenty years older than he looked, with his creased leathery skin, tanned by years of salt spray and sun. In fact, he had retired from the Royal Navy some years before the war, and then had knocked around Africa with his wife hunting big game. Their lounge was decorated with animal skins to prove it. He had been summoned back into the Navy to take charge of the naval dockyard at Trincomalee. It was there he was injured during the April raid of 1942, and was invalided out of the Service. How they came to settle in such an outlandish place was not made clear to me, but obviously they were happy there. They moved around on horseback, and still used their guns for hunting. We were surprised to learn that leopards were not uncommon in the district, and from then on we were much more watchful when rambling along the jungle paths.

On one such ramble we came across a lone man carrying out a task which must rank as one of the most peaceful in the world. Peaceful, that is, for the human race, but not for the prey who would end up skewered with a pin. He was a butterfly catcher. He had been walking the rain forests with his giant sized net for some thirty years, irrespective of the passing of wars. His sponsors were museums throughout the world. Nowadays, with so many butterfly parks around I daresay those beautiful insects have a better chance of survival.

For anyone visiting Ceylon, visits to both the Peradiniya Gardens, near Kandy, and the Hakgala Gardens, near Nuwara Eliya, are a must. Both supply Kew Gardens and other botanical gardens with tropical plants, and are laid out in magnificent natural settings.

It was unfortunate that only three of us were able to complete our leave as poor old Tony was stricken with a fever and we had to leave him in hospital in Kandy.

Chapter 8

Our return to China Bay coincided with the arrival of the north-westerly monsoon across the Bay of Bengal. It did not peter out until the end of May. The monsoon periods brought mixed blessings. It often meant that flying was cancelled for the day. It meant also that we got soaked with rain rather than perspiration. In June the sun was again master of the heavens. On the eighth of the month we bade farewell to our old CO Connie. He had served the squadron well and was now being promoted to Wing Commander and posted to India. His replacement seemed keen to befriend the erks, telling us that he hoped in the not too distant future to lead us into action in Burma.

On the 13th came the surrender of all enemy forces in North Africa, followed within days by the invasion of Sicily and the relief of the besieged island of Malta, whose residents had suffered for three and a half years the worst continual aerial bombardment of anywhere in the wartorn world.

The 17th marked for me three years spent in the RAF.

The camera club was now running smoothly, and new recruits meant that use of the darkroom needed to be rationed. One of those who had joined recently was a lugubrious engine fitter from Yorkshire by the name of Freddie Kemp. Freddie was not exactly a bundle of fun; in fact, he was a typically dour Yorkshireman. He was inconspicuous in the squadron except for one thing: he was hung like a rhino!

At first, Freddie seemed oblivious of the one physical asset that projected him inches beyond other male mortals. We often wondered whether his girl friend in Bradford, to whom he wrote regularly, sending photographs he had printed, was aware of what might be coming to her one day. So well known did LAC Kemp become in the squadron that when he was seen to be heading for the showers others would grab their towels and hasten that way also, just to get a sideways glance at the wondrous object glistening in the spray. Soon, any

52

cylindrical object measuring a foot or more came to be called a Freddie, and cucumbers were never alluded to in any other way. It was no wonder he walked with a loping gait, and wore the longest shorts in the squadron!

Around this time I was surprised to receive a letter from an old friend and next door neighbour from far distant North London. It was posted in Ceylon!

Bill, a wireless operator in the RAF, had been posted down to a new jungle airstrip some fifty miles inland from China Bay called Vavuniya. By pure chance a football team from 273 Squadron was due to play RAF Vavuniya the very next week. I managed to squeeze myself on to the team's lorry for the dusty journey inland through the scrubland and jungle to the west. Vavuniya was near to Anuradapura, the largest of the ruined cities of ancient Ceylon, said at the height of its power, some seven hundred years ago, to have been home to five million inhabitants.

Eventually, I tracked down Bill, who was not aware of my intended visit and whom I had not seen for more than two years. It was he who had introduced me to his cousin Doris with whom I was becoming more closely involved through our exchange of correspondence. I learnt of things that had happened at home about which I was not aware. Doris had been drafted into the Foreign Office, because of her fluent French and knowledge of German. She was involved in secret communications with the Maquis, the French resistance movement, about which I was not aware, and was later to become involved with the plans to invade Normandy.

That was the only occasion on which I was to see Bill whilst we were both in that part of Ceylon, but we were to meet up again on many occasions when we were both posted back to the Colombo area.

In the early hours of 19 July we were duly awakened by the wailing of the air raid siren. Expecting it to be merely a practice turnout instigated by some malicious minded headquarters officer we were surprised to hear the droning of an alien aircraft. Our Hurricanes took off but were unable to make contact with what was probably a Japanese reconnaissance sea plane. It was the first incursion of our airspace by the enemy since the Ceylon raids fifteen months previously. It was a reminder that we were still involved in a war which increasingly had seemed to us to apply only to other parts of the world.

By the end of July rumours were astir that 273 Squadron would be returning to Ratmalana, as number 17 Squadron were being moved down to China Bay for a well earned rest from operational service in Burma. On 17 August the ground personnel of 17 Squadron completed their long journey by train down the east coast of India, and by the end of the month their aircraft moved in as we prepared to move out again to Ratmalana. I don't think there were any tears shed about leaving China Bay for the last time.

Chapter 9

By the end of August 1943 number 273 Squadron's Hurricanes were back in Ratmalana, and we ground crews were glad to be back in familiar surroundings, close to Colombo and the beach at Mount Lavinia. The atap billets, spaced out between palm trees which provided welcome shade, were much the same, but unwelcome four-legged residents had moved in to the rafters.

Rats are tolerant towards human beings, particularly if they leave bits of food lying around. This toleration is not reciprocated by the human animal, especially when they keep him awake at night chasing one another around the bed spaces. Often, boots would be sent flying during this cavorting.

In the next bed to me was a jovial Lancastrian named Gordon, but always known as Gummy because he no longer had any teeth of his own. His capacity for the amber fluid was legend, and on beer nights the NAAFI would resound to his impersonation of a certain music hall comedian. In the cause of reality he would remove his dentures. They came out at night too, residing in a plate on top of his locker, grinning sepulchrally at all who passed by. The first thing Gummy did each morning was to reach out for his plateful of teeth.

After one particular beer night Gummy hazily stretched out a groping hand from beneath his mozzy net only to find his gnasher plate was empty.

'Who the bleeding hell's nicked my teeth?' yelled Gummy, having checked his bald gums to make sure that he had not forgotten to take them out whilst under the influence the previous night.

'Who do you think would want your poxy pearlies, Gummy?' responded Brummy.

Even Gummy had to admit the possibility was unlikely. So suspicion pointed towards our unwanted four-footed billet mates.

Already several attempts had been made to catch them, and ingenious traps had been devised to deal with the scourge. But some of the rats had grown so big and strong, fuelled by food left lying around, that they had been known to limp off on three legs taking the trap with them. The rodents seemed able to reproduce quicker than we could kill them off.

Some sympathy was generated towards Gummy, to the extent that all bedspaces were searched, and the floor cleared of boots and extraneous items. After all, Gummy had quite a reputation for flatulence, and without his teeth to masticate his fodder could become even more untenable after meals!

Searching down and around drew a blank; so they could only have gone out of the door, or upwards.

Lofty Lewis was nearest to the roof, and he it was who spotted the wandering gnashers grinning down from a cross-beam.

'Thank Christ for that,' said Gummy, as the rest of us sighed with relief. 'The buggers have been chewing them,' he moaned. That did not deter him from popping them in his mouth as he trudged off towards the cookhouse.

Apart from rats there were also occasional invasions from six-legged pests. One afternoon I was lying on my 'pit', which happened to be next to the doorway, at the jungle end, when I spotted the vanguard of an army of ants marching resolutely, ten abreast, towards the entrance. Leaping on to the floor I could see the column snaking its way out of the jungle towards the hut. If they reached the bed they would spread throughout the billet.

Petrol would have done the trick, but none was readily available. So it had to be a rapid conflagration of the *Ceylon Times* that I was reading when rudely alerted to the invasion. It did the trick. The invasion was averted, and the soldier ants retreated in disarray back into the bush.

As the ants retreated so too had the Italians. On 18 August Messina fell to the Eighth Army, and the invasion of the 'Italian Boot' took place soon after, leading to the surrender of the Italian forces on 8 September. We ignorant erks thought that meant the whole of Italy up to the Alps would be open to the northward advance of Montgomery's men, but the Germans had other ideas, realising the need to bolster their soft European under-belly. However, Naples fell to the Allies at the end of the month; but then the going became much tougher as the Germans dug in at Messina. The war in Europe was far from over yet, and in our part of the world the prospects seemed never ending. Perhaps we were enjoying ourselves too much to want it to end.

One of the enjoyments, around the 20th of the month, but for officers only, was the sighting of a contingent of WRNS stepping ashore in Colombo. This event roughly coincided with the return of the Eastern Fleet from its bases in East Africa, where it had been since the Ceylon raids, to Trincomalee.

Most of the erks and squaddies had not seen a white woman for a very long time, and the sight of skirts and stockings led to wolf whistling and drooling; but with odds at 500 to 1 it was only officers who would stand any chance of actually making physical contact. One exception was Bill, always the ladies' man, who had chanced to be posted, around the same time, to a radar station in the suburbs of Colombo, close to where a contingent of Wrens was billeted. I don't know how much physical contact there was, but there were boastings of having shared showers after a hard game of badminton!

Many years on I met up with one of the forty or so WRNS who were posted to Ceylon. She assured me that they were not just comforts for the troops but performed key jobs as wireless operators in Naval Headquarters, Colombo. Of course, she had the time of her life and remembers Ceylon with nostalgia. In her opinion the Wrens were always treated with respect by men in the armed forces.

As with many serving in Ceylon, the mountains of the central region provided a magnet when leaves were due. The sheer magnificence of the views of towering crags and waterfalls left a lasting impression.

At the end of October Bill, Pedlar, Mo and I took what I expected to be for me a last fourteen days' leave in the hills.

It was 26 October when our quartet set off soon after dawn, catching the bus to Ratnapura in the foothills of the mountain massif. The market town is best known for its semi-precious stones which are sieved from the rivers nearby. I bought a topaz and an aquamarine for presents to take home to England. The folks were very trusting, for we stayed in a guest house where there was a showcase of jewels in our room which had no more than a flimsy lock to secure the top, and tiny pieces of jewellery could be prized out of cracks in the floorboards.

Our target by road was some thirty miles further inland, a Rest House in a small village named Balihuloya, nestling beneath towering cliffs, where we were booked for the night prior to starting our climb on foot up to 7,000 feet above sea level at Horton Plains. Rain was falling heavily, as it can do only in the tropics, as we covered the last part of the first day by taxi to the comfortable Rest House where we were glad to dry out and enjoy a good meal before turning in to bed soon after dusk.

Luckily for us the sun rose into a clear sky the following morning, the shafts of light shimmering through the raindrops still upon the leaves from the previous night giving the whole valley a fairylike setting. After a good breakfast we set off on the upward path with a spring in our step, undaunted by the prospect of climbing one mile vertically.

By midday we were barely halfway, and the sun was beating down on our sweating bodies. Shade became sparser as we toiled upwards, but still the mountains towered above us.

But then, when exhaustion was about to claim us, we spotted the first signs of civilisation – the perimeter of a tea plantation. We knew salvation was near at hand, for we had only to follow the paths of the leaf pickers to reach the central collecting point where the freshly picked leaves would be laid out to dry on shelves of netting.

Near to the drying sheds was our Shangri La, the planter's bungalow. The plantation manager was an Indian of impressive stature and a university accent. He was amazed to see four white men approaching from the path leading up from the valley way below, and greeted us with a welcoming smile.

'You must be exhausted,' he exclaimed, 'come and sample our tea; we produce here the best in the world.' As we downed cup after cup, served by his boys, we were quite prepared to verify his claim.

Most of Ceylon's tea estates, which provide the backbone of the country's economy, were above the 5,000 feet level, where the air was cooler and the rainfall plentiful. Arguably, it was tea from Ceylon that kept up the morale of the severely rationed Britishers as they suffered the nightly bombings of the Luftwaffe. Every serviceman in Ceylon was permitted to send home one pound of tea, packed neatly in its little square box, every month. My own mother, of course, was very grateful to receive this boost to her meagre ration: so too was my future mother-in-law, and it is my belief that this inexpensive gift stood me in good stead in her affections in later years.

From the tea estate it was a fairly flat four miles across the plateau to the Rest House at Horton Plains which held a particular place in the hearts of Pedlar, Mo and myself who had been there before. Bill, whose first visit it was, was equally enchanted. The log fire at night, the rolling plains outside, interlaced with gurgling streams, might easily have been anywhere in the more remote parts of the British Isles.

On this occasion we were not alone in the Rest House, for, unlikely as it may seem, there was a trio of brigadiers also staying there. How the Army was able to spare three men of such exalted rank at the same time we would never know. We could hardly expect to be on chatting terms with brass hats in the Army, apart from asking them to pass the saltcellar at mealtimes, but their conversation was often along the same lines as we underlings, bemoaning the fact that someone else had not earned their promotion: in their case to major general, as opposed to corporal.

We spent three nights on Horton Plains, during which time we visited World's End, a place which would be a favourite for suicides as the cliffs drop sheer for more than two thousand feet. The view would have been fantastic had it not been for clouds rising up from the valley below.

From Horton Plains we descended some three miles to the railway at Ohiya station, 5,820 feet above sea level. There were no trains due so we made our way down alongside the track, a further one thousand feet, over four miles to the small town of Haputale, perched on a ridge between the mountains. Both the main road and the railway made use of this ridge. We had booked in at the Buena Vista Hotel, where our suitcases had been sent on by bus before setting out on our climb from Balihuloya. Once again the terrain was covered in cloud, but we were more than ready to get our heads down after a day's trudge of fifteen miles.

With the clouds still obscuring views the next morning we decided to push on down to Badulla, the terminus of the railway that crosses the central mountains, and some two thousand feet below Haputale. The town of Badulla is about the same size, and at the same height above sea level, as Kandy in the north of the mountain massif. Whilst Kandy is an ancient town and a religious centre devoted to Buddhism, Badulla was developed more recently by the European settlers. Many had prospered from the tea and coffee plantations, and money had been forthcoming to build a sizeable Anglican church.

It had been our intention to scale the nearby mountain, which at 6,666 feet dominated the town. However, the summit was still shrouded in cloud and intermittent drizzle was persisting. So, switching our plans, we decided to head upstream to the Danhilda Falls, some five miles up a narrow and densely foliaged valley from Badulla.

Three young boys attached themselves to our expedition, claiming to be guides, and for a few cents were useful in carrying our packs. Unfortunately for Pedlar and myself they also had a mischievous turn of mind. We were not quick enough to stop one of them hurling a branch into what turned out to be a very large swarm of hornets suspended from an overhanging bough. Not surprisingly these vicious insects did not take kindly to being disturbed in their slumbers and were quite swift in seeking retribution. Pedlar and I were not aware of what had caused the boys to race ahead before being stung on the ankles with the intensity of a bayonet thrust. I suffered an additional sting as I instinctively swiped the beast with my hand.

The falls of Danhinda, one of many in Ceylon in excess of one hundred feet, were magnificent; but the pleasure of seeing them was blunted by the excruciating pain of the stings. For a full twenty-four hours we suffered, wanting to do nothing more than lie on our beds.

Our attempts to scale Mount Namanakuh were thwarted at every turn, firstly by stings, then by the weather, and also by the lack of reliable information about paths. After two nights in Badulla we abandoned the climb and set off by bus on the thirty-five mile journey across the Uva plains and up into the mountains again to Nuwara Eliya.

After four years of war public transport in Ceylon was beginning to show the strain of the unavailability of replacement parts. Additional pressure had been applied by the influx of thousands of servicemen. Also, the buses in the interior were constantly toiling up and down mountain roads, so it was not surprising that our bus broke down after about ten miles, in the middle of nowhere. It was a beautiful spot to admire the views across the plain, with the backdrop of the mountains beyond; but it seemed to us that we might be there all day.

The problem was solved by the driver flagging down the bus approaching from the opposite direction. As the ensuing altercations between the drivers were conducted in local dialect I had no means of knowing how our bus driver persuaded the Badulla bus driver to turn his bus around and turf out all his passengers; but that is what happened!

It suited us, of course, but I can't imagine the reactions of the Badulla-bound passengers who were left standing on the roadside as we had been. It was probably solved this way because there were more of us heading towards Nuwara Eliya. Petrol must have also been a problem because we ran dry some ten miles short of our destination. Presumably the bus had enough in the tank to have reached Badulla, but not enough to get back to Nuwara Eliya over the

60

mountain pass. We had had enough of bus travel for the day, and so abandoned ship when a tea estate lorry came along the way we were wanting to go and obliged with a lift. Lorry drivers were usually helpful towards stranded servicemen.

I would never tire of Nuwara Eliya and its surrounding countryside, probably because it was reminiscent of the English Lake District where I had spent a memorable holiday in 1937. At 6,200 feet above sea level the climate was more amenable too. The standard of service at the Maysland Guest House, where I had stayed before, was well up to standard, with comfortable beds, and still a line of white jacketed boys serving curry at dinner time.

For Bill it was his first time in Nuwara Eliya and he was equally enraptured. The next day we initiated him in the traditional scaling of Mount Pedro, the highest point in Ceylon, which, to prove our fitness, we ran up most of the 2,100 feet in under the hour. For once we were rewarded with clear blue skies at the top, so it was possible to scan out across most of the island: a panorama well worth the effort of the climb.

The Grand Hotel was close to our guest house, and provided a bar and entertainment, in the shape of a billiard table, whenever we were not out exploring during our three-day stay. Nuwara Eliya boasted the only brewery in Ceylon, but the great influx of servicemen over the previous two years, with their prolific thirsts, had greatly exceeded output. Even the Grand Hotel, almost next door, could not get sufficient supplies.

Fortunately, the bus we boarded for the three-hour journey to Kandy seemed in better shape than the one from Badulla; it needed to be to negotiate the Ramboda Pass, with its descent of 3,400 feet, and a seemingly endless succession of hairpin bends.

As we needed to return to Ratmalana the following day we decided to tolerate one night in the Services' Rest Camp. We would put up with the clanging of the temple bells in the nearby Buddhist temple.

61

Chapter 10

Although the camp at Ratmalana seemed much the same on our return there were indications that things were going to happen. We had been detailed to undergo a three day toughening up course, which had been nicknamed a Commando Assault course. Feeling pretty fit after fourteen days leave this presented no problems, but probably indicated that we could be on our way to Burma before long. There were also rumours that we would soon be receiving Spitfires to replace our ageing Hurricanes.

On the night of 12 November there was a rare air raid warning. This time it was not a false alarm: a Japanese 'recce' seaplane was shot down in flames just off the coast, but not by one of 273 Squadron's planes. In fact, we had yet to claim an enemy plane, although we had lost one or two of our own in accidents, apart from the one shot down in the raids of Easter 1942.

The north-easterly monsoon set in in November. Some of the effects of monsoon weather were good, and some bad. The good were the topping up of tanks and reservoirs that provided our daily showers, and conditions were also good for surfing off the beach at Mount Lavinia. Conditions were often unfavourable for flying, thereby giving us some time off. On the debit side the airfield dispersal point became a quagmire, and the billet roofs usually leaked.

A further indication of the stream-lining of the squadron, prior to moving towards active service, was the posting of personnel who were either not fully fit medically, or who were over thirty years of age. My old friend Mo, pushing thirty-two, was posted to a maintenance unit across the other side of the airfield, entitled Ceylon Reserve Aircraft Pool, in short CRAP. I was not to see Mo again until after the war when on honeymoon in 1946 near his home town of Glastonbury.

Also posted, on medical grounds, was a Brummy fitter who was always known as Hup Hup. The nickname was onomatopoeic, on account of involuntary noises he often made, at the same time as stamping his feet. It was a nervous affliction harking back to the time of his escape from Singapore. Clearly it would not have been a good thing for him to be exposed again to possible enemy action. He was a nice enough chap, but his involuntary noises were often disturbing for those sharing his billet.

Once again Christmas was coming round. It was always a sad time when one thought of Christmases past, before the war, when as a boy one would wake at dawn in anticipation of presents to come, and family gatherings; not to mention the certainty of a very special feast. For three years now there had been no exchanging of presents, and thoughts of home and family generated anxiety that they might not be well, or able to manage the harshness of wartime conditions. However, I was always confident that my mother, ever resourceful, would be coping with whatever adversity crossed her path. Somehow it never occurred that she might be worrying about me.

On 15 December the squadron received its Christmas present with the arrival of the new planes, Spitfires Mark V, no less. We could now claim that we really were a fighter squadron, ready to do battle wherever needed. Our ageing

Bullock race round the perimeter of RAF Ratmalana. Boxing Day 1943.

Hurricanes had served us well, but the extra knots provided by the Spitfires would be an asset; also, they were the favourites of all pilots. Airframe fitters, like me, favoured them too, for there was no fabric to contend with, or inspection panels for electricians. I had once suffered seven days 'jankers' at China Bay because an electrician had not secured his inspection panel properly, and it had fallen off in flight.

Over the Christmas period training was suspended, and the likelihood of a Japanese air attack had become a thing of the past, so all the squadron personnel could concentrate on the festivities. Only the cooks had a harder time; but I expect it relieved the usual monotony for them. Certainly the extra rations and portions were appreciated by the erks. The cookhouse was decorated, as was the NAAFI and many of the billet huts, some of whose residents used a great deal of ingenuity and imagination in carrying out the transformations. The winner of a crate of beer, presented by the CO, was B Flight's replica of an old English pub, the realism of which was almost nostalgic.

The big attraction on Boxing Day was the squadron bullock races, held on the dispersal road. It was a hilarious occasion that seemed to be enjoyed by all excepting the bullocks, who had never been used to towing their carts at anything more than a pedestrian pace. The most successful ploy to gain acceleration was for the jockey, seated on his cart, to grip the bullock's scrotum between the big toe and the next one. When approaching the winning post a sharp tug on the bullock's bollocks produced some quite unexpected results! As usual, the real winners were the bookies, and the small boys who collected up the droppings afterwards to sell for fertilizer.

Two cricket matches were played, in spite of the semi-inebriated state of many of the team. In fact, during my time in Ceylon, as a regular member of the 273 Squadron XI, I spent a large part of my spare time, and often normal working time too, playing cricket. At other times it was often tennis, or table tennis, mostly with my friend Bill.

On 28 December came the news that the German battleship *Scharnhorst* had been sunk. This may not have been a significant naval victory, but it was a great morale booster as the old year drew to a close. The *Scharnhorst* had suffered a great deal of harassment (or should it have been Harrisment, in recognition of the chief of Bomber Command?) during four years of war, and, though often damaged, had seemed unsinkable.

So AD 1943 faded out with the customary booze-up to see in the New Year, followed by a hangover the next morning. Last New Year's Day four of us had seen in spectacularly from the summit of Adam's Peak, but this year there did not seem to be the urge for a grandiose gesture. Nevertheless, the war news was clearly more optimistic, as 1944 dawned, and we felt more hopeful of the prospect of maybe seeing Blighty again before too much longer.

In the middle of January I reached the great age of twenty-four. Although one or two more Xs appeared at the end of Doris's letters from North London I had no serious thoughts of getting married when I returned to the old country. My brief loving of Tau Fong, during the escape from Malaya, seemed now little more than a sex romp, but stirred my loins from time to time at night.

On 29 January, I and a few mates were invited to a party in a large private house near to the aerodrome, owned by a wealthy Sinhalese.

It was my first experience of socialising in the house of a non-European, and I did experience a certain awkwardness. I suppose it was because I had been brought up to think that the British were superior to any other race on earth; my mother had instilled this basic knowledge into me at an early age. During the evening it became apparent to me that this Sinhalese family was mentally and educationally superior to me, and so my mother's teachings had to go out of the window. I had not adjusted to my new outlook on life before it was time to return to camp.

The 366th day of 1944 was for me remarkable for only one thing, and that occurred within the last hour of the Leap Year's Day. I had just returned to the darkened billet, all quiet except for unmelodious snores, and had crawled beneath my mozzy net when the whole bed began to shake: in fact, it was more of a judder. Having just consumed a few jars of local brew I thought it might be the after effects; or perhaps my mates were playing some sort of practical joke. Indeed, it was my first, and only, experience of an earthquake. Although the epicentre proved to be some six hundred miles away it was an eerie experience.

One morning early in March a four-engined York aircraft, the first of its kind I had ever seen, touched down at Ratmalana bearing the newly appointed Supreme Commander of the South East Asia Area. Lord Louis Mountbatten was on his way to take up the reins of office in Colombo. It happened to be the day of the Ceylon football cup final, to be held on the Galle Face green near the centre of Colombo. It was there that one of number 30 Squadron's Hurricanes had crash landed during the April 1942 raid. On this day the green had been set up for the big occasion. The RAF was to do battle with the Ceylon Light

Infantry in the final.

Service vehicles converged from all parts of the island for the big day. Our squadron had a vested interest in the RAF team as two of our cooks were in the side that had won through in earlier rounds against both Army and Navy teams.

It proved to be a most unusual match. The Ceylon Light Infantry were smaller men and with one exception, their European commanding officer, who wore boots, all played barefooted. The officer played centre defence, controlling his men rather like a traffic policeman. The fleetness of foot of the local islanders let them run rings around the RAF men, enabling them to score first. It was not until the second half that the RAF players, by then 3-1 down, got the measure of the situation by using their greater weight and aggressiveness to advantage, eventually running out winners 4-3.

To everyone's surprise the Supremo, as Lord Louis came to be known, arrived at the ground at half time, having only touched down on the island that very morning. It would seem that he was deliberately setting out on a policy that he pursued throughout his command, of being seen as much and as often as possible, by as many men as possible in the South East Asia war area.

It was soon after the Cup Final that Lord Louis came to see 273 Squadron. There was no formal parade; the Station Warrant Officer was simply told to gather as many men as possible in a semi-circle at the dispersal point. Someone produced a tool box for Mountbatten to stand on to give us his pep talk, and to outline his plans to defeat the enemy. What he had to tell us did have the effect of instilling a realisation of being part of the war effort, shaking off the feeling of defeatism that had gripped us since the fall of Singapore.

There was little doubt that we would soon be thrust into the active service area to the north, away from the backwaters of Ceylon. Judging from the stories of the men from those squadrons sent down to the Emerald Isle for a rest, our prospects were not likely to be envied. The monsoons were due in Assam in the spring, and Lord Louis had already decreed there should be no let-up in applying pressure on the enemy.

Indeed, it was the enemy who, in the spring of 1944, was advancing through the Burmese jungle westwards towards the glittering goal of Calcutta, and the expanse of India beyond. The hopes of the Japanese, at that time, that resistance would collapse once the Ganges Delta had been crossed were not entirely ill founded. Many in India had long wanted independence from the British. Perhaps assistance from the Japanese would succeed in prising the Imperial grip on the sub-continent: a certain Mr Bose thought so. On the other hand there were leaders trusted by the millions of Hindus and Moslems who had witnessed the subjugation of a large part of China by the Japanese, and who had little relish to go down the same road. There was nothing to be gained by jumping out of the frying pan into the fire.

Firstly, the Japanese army had to contend with a newly appointed leader of the 14th Army, General Slim, who was well liked by his men, who had bestowed upon him the nickname Uncle Bill. His next in command, General Stilwell, in charge of the American Forces, was less popular with his underlings, earning the nickname of Vinegar Joe.

Chapter 11

In March 1944, more than a year after first applying to remuster as a flight engineer, I was summoned to undertake a suitability test. In fact, it was little more than a formality, and I was told to get in as much flying experience as possible before being sent to begin flight training, presumably in the UK. Indeed, there was not much scope on a fighter squadron to gain flying experience as we only had single-seater planes. However, I felt elated that I would be seeing some action after two years spent in Ceylon. Seemingly, after four and a half years of war I had become conditioned to the prospect of the global conflict continuing indefinitely.

In the meantime life at Ratmalana went on peacefully enough whilst we awaited the expected move to Burma, particularly now that the Squadron was being re-equipped with Mark VIII Spitfires. Much of my spare time was taken up with photography, and under the expert guidance of Mo Brock and Pedlar Palmer, both of whom had had professional experience of photography, I was getting quite proficient at both taking and processing films. The folks at home were always pleased to receive snaps with my letters, and I was beginning to accumulate quite a sizeable album as a result of my labours in the tiny darkroom some of us had set up under a water tank on the camp. Most of our work was carried out after dusk. It was hot enough then in the confined space about six feet square, but unbearable during the daytime.

Supplies of material such as printing paper and films were ever a problem, and we were always on the lookout for anything photographic when visiting Colombo.

Another source of entertainment was the regular classical music concerts that were put on by Len (Rommel) Smith, assisted by Ralph Ambrose. Although I had always considered myself in the lowbrow category of music, more jazz and dance band than arias and orchestras, I was beginning to be educated into classical music. The organisers were clearly dedicated to their music and must have worked miracles to acquire their collection of records. In this respect our medical officer, Doc Gordon, gave much assistance and a great deal of his spare time.

Luckily, I did not have cause to bother the sick bay overmuch during my first three years abroad. Somehow I managed to avoid being infected by the dreaded mosquito. Perhaps it was only the non-poisonous males of the species that bit me.

In the earlier days in Ceylon I had once been laid low with some sort of fever. Crawling to the sick bay, where the medical orderly recorded a temperature of 104 degrees, I was whisked off smartly to the hospital at Dehiwala. I don't think the medicos in the hospital knew what had laid me low. When I was discharged after a week in dock my discharge paper merely stated that I had suffered from a common cold!

I recall a hasty visit to the sick bay one dark night when I ventured outside the billet to relieve myself against a tree. I had no idea what I had trodden upon, but whatever it was resented being subjected to the sole of my sandal and retaliated with a sharp nip in the ankle. In great pain I limped the hundred yards or so to the sick bay where the orderly spotted two punctures in flesh around the ankle bone, about a half inch apart, which were probably inflicted by a snake. With no idea what sort of snake he had to assume that it was poisonous. It was important to keep me upright and conscious while the area was cut out and the resulting hole filled with permanganate of potash crystals. Without anaesthetics, it was not an operation I would wish to have repeated. After that I was much more careful where I trod in the undergrowth!

In April, whilst awaiting the expected orders to move northwards, I had the chance to take a few days' leave. Indeed, I had not expected another opportunity to roam free in the hinterland of Ceylon, but the squadron Orderly Office indicated it would be at least a month before the advance party moved off from Ratmalana.

There were two others in 'Λ' Flight who also had the chance to take seven days' leave, and so we hastily made our plans to journey up into the mountains. Tony had previously accompanied Mo, Pedlar and myself on leave; in fact, it was he who had fallen lame during the ascent of Adam's Peak. Again, on a later expedition, he was taken ill with malaria and we had to leave him in an up-country hospital.

Tony was a well educated man, with a steady pre-war job in a well known bank. I had played cricket with him several times, but his reputation for accident proneness often let him down, and I cannot remember his prowess on the field of play ever matching up to his potential. For all that, he was good company, always with a wealth of stories to suit almost any occasion. He was involved with amateur dramatics before the war, mainly, it would seem, for the opportunities it offered to mix with female company. I vividly recall him relating one particular love scene, when dressed in tights on stage he needed to turn his back on the audience because of a raging erection!

The third member of our little expedition was an erudite engine fitter named Bill Somers. Bill was more a friend of Tony's than mine, towering nearly a head above Tony's diminutive 5 feet 3 inches. With his stentorian voice and educated repartee I had always considered him to be officer material. He also had the right sort of moustache for the job.

We had all been to Horton Plains before, loving the peace and tranquillity of the guest house, as well as the temperate climate. Our plan of approach to the mountain massif this time was to make the ascent from the south using firstly the train and then the local buses.

From the railway station at Ratmalana we boarded the southbound evening train towards Galle, the line following round the southern coast of Ceylon as it curved eastward towards the southernmost extremity, Dondra Head. It was from near there that the Oscars and Mitsubishis of Admiral Nagumo's task force, shielded by Zero fighters, had taken off from their fleet carriers on the fateful Easter Sunday of 1942.

Near to the headland the railway terminated at the small town of Matara. It was here that we put up overnight at the rather seedy guest house.

As the sun rose the following morning the three of us grabbed a hasty breakfast, and our haversacks, in time to board the bus bound for Haputale. At least we were in time to get seats in the open-sided vehicle before it filled up with fellow travellers, often clutching baskets laden with vegetables or even livestock, gesticulating and frequently arguing in a tongue that meant nothing to us, but added to the colourfulness of the scene.

As the bus chugged along the coastal plains with its sweating load, through the towns of Tangalla and Hambantota, we were filled with trepidation that the overloaded vehicle would not be able to tackle the climb of nearly 5,000 feet to Haputale. But we had great faith in the endurance of Ceylon's mostly ancient buses which always seemed to reach their destinations in the end.

Our faith was not misplaced, and by early afternoon we, or rather the bus driver, had negotiated the endless hairpins and we were stretching our aching limbs on terra firma at Haputale.

'Packs on backs,' commanded Tony, 'it's a good twelve miles uphill from here.' As we set off in the direction of Horton Plains the track dwindled to a rough path as we negotiated the climb. I expect that Bill Somers was thinking along the same lines as me, hoping that Tony's unpredictable knees did not give out *en route*, and that we would not finish up carrying him.

This time all was well as the welcome sight of Horton Plains guest house came into view, bathed in the mellow light of the setting sun.

Abdul, the guest house manager, remembered me, and what little one could see of his weatherbeaten face surrounding his voluminous black moustache broke into a welcoming smile. He showed us to our rooms which looked out across the valley that reminded us so much of the Yorkshire Moors.

After a shower and a meal we adjourned to the lounge where a welcoming log fire crackled in the hearth. To our surprise, seated on either side of the blaze were two gentlemen, both in early middle age, one in khaki shorts and shirt and the other dressed in a check shirt and grey shorts. Both were holding glasses, with bottles beside their chairs.

Both turned their heads towards the three of us as we entered the room. The civilian in the check shirt was the first to speak. Clearly he had put to good use the nearly empty whisky bottle by his chair.

'Come in, chaps,' he slurred in a high pitched voice, 'pull up chairs and join us for a drink.' He spoke with an Oxbridge accent, and judging by his weatherbeaten clean shaven face had been resident in the tropics for some while.

As we settled into our well worn wicker chairs he continued, waving his glass in the flickering light of the fire.

'I'm Cedric Harvey, been out here tea planting for years. My place is twelve miles down to the north from here. Had my wife out here until the bloody Japs came and bombed Colombo; now she is back in Reigate with the two nippers. Bloody lonely without them. Might be like it for years till I can join them.'

Turning to his friend he continued. 'This is the Captain; Frank by name. Used to run an import business in Colombo until the war came and his business faded away leaving him nothing to do but join the local Ceylon Light Infantry.'

The Captain sported a luxurious black moustache, which made up for his lack of hair on top. He spoke with a more mellow, less inebriated, but equally educated voice. 'I am up with Cedric on leave for a week. We've come up here with our rods for a couple of days fishing. Caught bugger all to-day. Any of you lads fish?'

Tony and I shook our heads. Bill, acting as our spokesman, said he had done a little back home. 'Tony, Ken and I are all RAF ground staff, just up here because of our love of mountains and the freedom of walking around sampling the solitude and silence of the jungle. Aeroplanes are such noisy things.'

The evening passed convivially, with many stories of home exchanged, plus a few risqué, or positively filthy, yarns thrown in. By the time the last embers glowed in the ashes Cedric was practically paralytic and needed to be helped to his room. We three turned in too, for we had had a long tiring day.

The sun was well above the trees next morning as we tucked in to a traditional English breakfast. Cedric and the Captain joined us.

'We are going to head back this morning to Bogowantalawa, that's my estate down the valley,' said Cedric, having recovered remarkably well from the night before. 'Why don't you three join us there in a couple of days' time?'

We did not need any time to give consideration to the invitation; it had been years since any of us had spent any time in a private house.

So Cedric and the Captain headed northwards down the path to the tea estate that was home to Cedric, whilst we three trekked in the opposite direction towards World's End, the spectacular viewpoint some 3,000 feet above the plains below.

On the Tuesday morning we buckled on our back packs and set forth on the same twelve mile trek to Bogowantalawa. There was a sadness about leaving Horton Plains for what we knew must be the very last time. The haven of peace had been home from home for us on several occasions and would remain in my memory during the harder times that must lie ahead.

For some ten miles we walked the well defined path through the rain forest, under the canopy of green, until the light grew stronger as we neared the perimeter of Cedric's plantation. In themselves, tea bushes are rather boring plants, reminding me of the small privet hedge that my father used to trim most summer week-ends outside our family home in North London. Planted regimentally on the south-facing slopes they are not permitted to grow more than about four feet above the ground level, just high enough for the pickers to reach across the tops to pluck the leaves and throw them into the wicker baskets fastened to their backs. The women and girls who picked the leaves, bedecked in their colourful saris, enhanced the picturesque scene as they went about their monotonous task just to earn a very few dollars at the end of the day.

In the distance, lower down the hillside, we could make out the tea factory building, and beyond it the owner's bungalow.

A large black labrador came bounding towards us, barking furiously. Luckily for our ankles he pulled up short, seeming to sense that we had no evil intents. Following on behind came Cedric, a broad smile on his face, now apparently fully recovered from his Horton Plains hangover.

'You're just in time for tiffin, lads. You'll have a snifter first, of course,' was Cedric's cheery greeting. 'I see that Caesar has already made friends with you. I told him to expect three handsome RAF men.'

'You've got a nice place here,' commented Tony as we were met at the door of the bungalow by two boys in traditional white jackets.

'It's nice enough when I have guests here,' Cedric commented, 'but bloody lonely when there's only Caesar for company in the evenings. It's more than two years now since the wife and children left for England. I only hope this damned war is not going to last too much longer; I'm too old to join any of the services. In any case, the Government want me to keep the tea flowing through for the sake of the beleaguered population in the UK who need their cuppas to keep up morale.'

After being shown to our rooms, which were probably those once occupied by Cedric's family, we joined our host and Frank for tiffin. The Captain rose from his armchair, glass in hand, and greeted us cheerily.

'Did you come across any leopards on your way down from the plains?' said Frank.

'We've heard about leopards in these parts, but never seen one,' said Tony. 'I don't expect they thought we would make a good meal; that's if they really exist.'

'They exist all right,' said Cedric, 'but they would not attack where there is more than one person. If you are on your own in the jungle, it's as well to be armed.'

After tiffin we were shown by our host around the factory where the freshly picked green tea leaves were brought in at one end and exited at the other end in wooden boxes. The word factory one associates with noise and activity, but not in a tea plantation. The drying rooms consisted of row upon row of rough hessian racks upon which the leaves were spread out to dry naturally in the warm air. Even the workers glided around silently on their bare feet, not daring to utter a word within earshot of their sahibs.

In the grading room were a line of small bowls of cold tea ready for tasting by the boss. My thoughts were that Cedric's palate would have become insensitive to the bouquet of the tea on account of the whisky and brandy. However, a sniff and a look seemed to suffice.

The following day we bade farewell to the Captain who had to return to his unit in Colombo. As we reclined that evening on the balcony, after a memorable curry, the smoke from our cigarettes curling gently upwards towards the waxing moon, I could not help reflecting that we were witnessing also the evening of the British Raj, where the sun never sets on the red patches on the globe. Surely nothing would be quite the same again.

On the Thursday, after breakfast, we bade our host farewell. He was clearly sad to be left on his own again, with no English company, and we made promises to meet up again in England which we knew in our hearts would never come about; and so we set forth on the ten-mile trek to the railway at Hakgala.

The train terminated at Kandy where Mountbatten had decided to set up his headquarters for the South East Asia Command. One could not fault him for choosing this ancient capital of Lanka, with its holy places of worship, its tranquil lake teeming with holy fish, and the ever prevailing scent of fruit blossom wafting in the languid air.

We booked in for two nights at a cheap hotel and took one last look round this beautiful city, watching the holy elephants enjoying their daily scrub down in the river and the brightly saried pilgrims filing barefooted past the Shrine of the Buddha's Tooth.

Having chatted with two soldiers in the hotel bar that night we were able to arrange a lift in their army lorry for the following morning. Again, it was sad to be leaving the mountains behind us, for what we knew must be the last time, as the 15 cwt truck bounced its way towards Colombo and the heat of the coastal plains. However, there were the prospects of new adventures ahead as we reached the camp guardroom that night.

Chapter 12

The next morning it was back to work down at flight dispersal where our pilots were getting used to handling the newly acquired Spitfires Mark V. The whole place was buzzing with rumours. One always wondered where and how rumours started, but however they came about it always added spice to the boredom that often prevailed.

News of what was happening in the whole of the South East Asia Command became more reliable since the publication, by order of the Supremo, of a regular news-sheet. During April, and the time we were on leave up country, the Japs had been advancing steadily northwards, intending to break through to the Indian plains before the onset of the monsoon season. However, they were being held by stubborn resistance from the 14th Army, firstly at Imphal and later at Kohima. In the May news-sheet a great victory was being claimed at Kohima on what later came to be known as the battle for the tennis court at the Government residence.

At the time we tended to greet the 'great victory' as propaganda being broadcast for the sake of morale. For those of us who had experienced the Japanese conquest of Malaya and suffered the subsequent humiliations during 1942, the Japanese army had seemed invincible. However, we had witnessed the gradual build up of the Air Force, and Japanese aircraft were now conspicuous by their absence as reinforcements were moved more and more to counter the American carrier-borne incursions in the Pacific.

Air supremacy would win in the end, as was happening against the Luftwaffe in Europe. The ubiquitous Dakota aircraft, with umbrella protection from the likes of our Spitfires, were providing vital supplies to the 14th Army sections fighting for their lives in Assam. Indeed, by the end of May 1944 the Japanese advance had been halted, and General Slim was preparing for his counter-attack southwards as the enemy began to retreat.

In our own small way plans to move up to the front in Burma were under way also. The personnel of the two flights were being slimmed down to operational requirements. This was being carried out by posting the older men, which in practice meant over about twenty-five. My old mates Mo Brock, by now aged thirty-two, and Pedlar Palmer were amongst those being transferred to permanent maintenance units in Ratmalana. It heralded the breakup of friendships dating from the time of Singapore. It also meant the dissolution of our photographic club which we could not hope to sustain on active service.

Towards the end of May I spent my last day off in Colombo, mainly to bid farewell to Bill Hart. Because of his job in Signals he knew already about the imminent departure of 273 Squadron for Burma. As my next door neighbour in Muswell Hill I knew that we would meet up again some day, provided we both survived the war. I did not know then just how closely our lives would be intertwined. I could not know then that Bill would be my best man, not just once but three times over fifty years.

We ate together for the last time in the Services Club restaurant in the Fort, Colombo, and played there our last game of table tennis, a favourite pastime since first we became neighbours in 1939. We had played even when bombs were falling during the London blitz in 1940.

Our journey north was to be by train, apart, of course, from the two ferry crossings necessary to reach Chittagong in Assam some 1,500 miles away. It was to be the longest train journey of my life, and was to take all of fifteen days. It was as well that I liked trains; indeed, they had been something of a passion for as long as I could remember, probably inherited from my father who had spent much of his life collecting railway tickets. In my short-trouser days, as soon as I was allowed out with my friend from across the road, we would gravitate to the Great Northern main line about a mile from home. On summer days we would sit on the fence near the tunnel portals at New Southgate trying to guess what type of engine we could hear underground as it came towards us. My friend Cliff was more expert than me because his dad actually worked for the London North Eastern Railway Company at King's Cross.

To return to Ratmalana, the squadron was to move in two parts; the main party, of which I was one, would set off early in June. The Spitfires, with their pilots and skeleton ground staff, would remain at Ratmalana until we were ready to receive them in Chittagong.

Early in June we had packed up and were moved off by lorry to the local railway station at Mount Lavinia where a special train awaited us. It was already dark as the 273 train chugged slowly through Colombo central station and out again to the north. I had been that way before to Trincomalee in the north-west, Puttalam on the east coast, and of course, the climb up through the mountains from Polgahawela; but never had I journeyed due north towards Jaffna. In the small hours of the morning we passed the ancient ruined city of Anuradhapura which I had always meant to visit during my time in Ceylon, but now the chance was gone for ever. Beyond the one-time capital of the Kingdom of Lanka the line to Adam's Bridge, and beyond to India, veered to the west, and as dawn was breaking we crossed the causeway to the island of Mannar, and eased to a halt at the ferry jetty on the westernmost point.

It was a welcome break to stretch my legs aboard the boat for the two-hour crossing to the sub-continent. Adam's Bridge itself is no more than a string of tiny sandy islands that are deserted. What the connection is between Adam's Bridge and Adam's Peak I do not know, but it is probably to do with some mythical giant.

The landing point in India is named Dhanushkodi, which consists of nothing but a rail terminal in a desert of sand that projected into the Indian Ocean as if pleading for sustenance from the green and pleasant land beyond. It seemed the most inhospitable land I had ever seen.

As the sun rose in the sky the heat became almost unbearable as it reflected up from the barren ground. The carriages were spartan in the extreme, with wooden slats for seating and no provision for lying horizontal for the one night we would have to spend on the way to Madras.

Before long dehydration began to grip us by the throat before a halt was called in mid-morning at a depressing wayside halt. There was no water available, so tea was brewed in a sort of witches' cauldron, the water being provided by releasing the steam valve on the engine which responded with a roar of steaming liquid targeted on to a murky muslin bag filled with tea, likened by the lads to a bullock's bollock. The several gallons of turgid brown water were soon reduced by the whole squadron dipping their mugs into the liquid until only a muddy residue remained to be tipped onto the track. At least the water had been boiled!

Food that day was what was referred to as hard tack – one tin of bully beef and two hard biscuits more suitable for dogs, which unless dunked into the tea were a danger for those with dentures.

The sun set and rose again next day as the train jolted and jogged its way gently northwards. After some thirty hours we came across the first signs of civilisation, the overhead electric cables of the Madras suburban trains. It was a great relief to grind to a halt in the southern railway terminus of Madras.

Here we needed to transfer all our stores and equipment because of the change of gauge from 3½ feet to the British standard gauge 4 feet 8½ inches for the three day journey on to Calcutta. We stretched our legs before boarding lorries to take us into the city where we were to stay overnight in a transit camp.

The city of Madras, like all great Indian cities, teemed with milling millions, usually carrying bulging bundles, often on decrepit bicycles whilst chewing the habitual betel nut, the ruddy juice of which was expectorated into the gutters, staining them like blood. The European area of the city was shady and pleasant. Here we were able to satisfy pangs of hunger at the Services' canteen.

The next morning we were soon aboard the Indian Railways train heading north, pulled by a massive Pacific class engine, with its gleaming brass bell mounted on the boiler. The compartments on this standard gauge were more spacious but no more comfortable, with the same sort of slatted seats and backrest which hinged upwards forming a middle berth two feet or so beneath the wide luggage racks, thereby providing primitive sleeping accommodation for six men in each compartment.

At intervals the train would stop for the brew-up of tea and consumption of hard tack. From somewhere a football would be produced, and a nearby piece of ground would serve as a pitch for 'A' Flight versus 'B' Flight until the engine's whistle provided the full time signal, sending the footballers scampering back to board their coaches as the train began to gather speed. It was the only form of exercise we had during the three days before reaching the bustling Howra station in Calcutta, on the western bank of the Hooghly river.

I have memories of being locked into the compartment as the train made its way through the French colony of Pondicherry, technically neutral territory at that time on account of the puppet Vichy government in France. Maybe it was thought that someone might try to 'do a runner'.

The high bridge across the river Debi at Cuttack provided some excitement for it had been breached in 1942 by Japanese bombers, and the train had to negotiate very slowly a temporary girder structure that had been thrown across the gap.

The giant cantilever road bridge across the Hooghly river, to gain access to Calcutta, had not long been completed, and memories of the blitz in Blighty were renewed by the stationing of barrage balloons to protect the structure.

The three goods vans containing the squadron equipment and our heavy baggage did not need to be unloaded to continue the journey to Chittagong, our final destination, as the rail gauge was the same. With my love of railways I was one of six, including a corporal in charge, to volunteer to stay with the vans as travelling guards. For this purpose we were issued with rifles. It meant missing out on the opportunity of seeing something of Calcutta, but judging by reports of the effect of the Bengal famine it would not be a pretty sight, with dead and dying lying around the streets of the poorer parts.

Apart from us six guards the remainder would proceed by rail and ferry boat across the vast Ganges Delta to Chittagong. The distance the proverbial crow would fly was little more than two hundred miles, but it took them three days. For us, travelling in our two goods vans and a guard's van, frequently being shunted from one train to another, it took nearly a week, although we only needed to transfer the baggage once.

The train, with our three vans tacked onto the rear, headed north along the west bank of the Hooghly river, one of the many outlets to the sea of the Ganges, until we reached a rail crossing of the river. A small tank engine backed on to our vans and we were taken across the massive girder bridge to join another train on the eastern side. The driver invited us to travel on the footplate; for me this was one of the highlights of the war.

For more than a day we chugged across the flat plain of the delta, with little to see but mud huts and vultures wheeling in the sky. It was pleasant enough squatting on the open platform of the guard's van. For recreation we took pot shots at various targets that presented themselves.

On the second day there was the rare occurrence of a nearly complete eclipse of the sun. There was an eerieness as the daylight faded for a brief few minutes at midday.

On the third day we only travelled two miles, spending all day shunted on to an otherwise deserted siding while we waited for space on the Ganges train ferry. We could not see the ferry or the river from our siding which obviously had seen many a troop train judging by the piles of rotting excreta all along the centre of the marshalling yard tracks. Indeed, not a pleasant place to spend the day.

I had been waiting to experience the Ganges crossing by rail ferry, but in this I was thwarted for it was carried out at night. I was only just conscious of a lot of jolting going on. Next day the mighty Brahmaputra River was spanned by a massive bridge, and eventually we reached the terminus at Chittagong after fifteen successive days on railtracks.

By the time we reached the billets the main party had already been installed for three days and had appropriated all the best bed spaces. The *bashas* must have been constructed early in the war for they leaked profusely when it rained, and that seemed to be most of the time. Humidity was such that one's sweat dampened everything, even through the night. A container of salt, if left on the messroom table overnight, would just be salt water in the morning. One night whilst four of us were playing solo, because sleep was hard to achieve in the damp, we heard a low rumble and much shouting from the billet next door as it subsided to the ground under the weight of water on rotting bamboo poles. Fortunately, no one was hurt.

All in all Chittagong was a rather depressing part of the world, and I was glad that I spent only six weeks there. There was little to see or do in the small town. Indeed, I can only recall visiting it once. The airfield and quarters were extensive, with several units sharing the facilities. Among them were American airmen. It was the first time I had rubbed shoulders with our Allies. We got chatting to them in the mess where I was intrigued by their habit of using a knife only for cutting up food, after which they would transfer the fork to the right hand and use only that for the eating process. Often they would mix in their dessert with the meat course.

It did not assist good relations when we learnt that the US servicemen were receiving hardship allowances on top of pay already far superior to ours for doing the same job.

Towards the end of August we were told we would be moving further south down the coast to Cox's Bazar. It was the RAF's most forward airstrip at that time on the Arakan front and had been in the hands of the Japanese during 1942/43. Because of the possibility of enemy infiltration we were issued with rifles. I looked upon mine merely as an encumbrance, particularly as I was never any good at target practice owing to the astigmatism in my right eye. We were told to keep the bolt clean and separated from the breech, presumably so that in the event of the rifle being stolen it would be of little use to an enemy. I always had great difficulty in finding my bolt whenever it was needed, and eventually lost it altogether, which presented great problems when ultimately I had to hand it in.

I packed up my kitbag once again, but this time with little regret.

Chapter 13

The distance by boat from Chittagong to Cox's Bazar was roughly sixty miles. It made a pleasant change to move entirely by sea in a small steamer, some sixty feet long, that chugged steadily within sight of land at some ten knots.

The small village of Cox's Bazar, which aspired to be referred to as a port because of its proximity to a muddy creek, was founded in 1798 by Captain Hiram Cox of the East India Company. It was once occupied by Arkanese Buddhist immigrants from Myanmer, and has a mixed population speaking Bangla and Burmese. In more peaceful times it was renowned for its cottage

The local supermarket.

industries housing silk and cotton weavers as well as cigar makers; but many had fled in recent times when the Japanese army occupied the area, making use of the long sandy ridge for an aircraft runway. Now it had been recaptured by the 14th Army and our Spitfires were about to move in.

There was a happy atmosphere about the RAF camp at Cox's Bazar as we settled into the recently constructed *bashas* on a sandy ridge about a mile from the dispersal point next to the metal strip runway which ran alongside the sea shore.

Everywhere there was sand as far as the eye could see north and south. Indeed, the shoreline beach stretched for seventy-five miles, claiming to be the longest in the world.

There were none of the usual camp facilities. Fortunately, we had arrived just after the monsoon had worked itself out, so it was possible to bathe in a nearby stream of brackish water, which was quite a novelty. The 'lavatory' was merely a sort of slit trench over which one perched precariously, trying to hold one's breath for as long as possible. In fact, it became so unsavoury that most men just scooped out a hole anywhere in the sand when the need arose. There were always plenty of insects and scavengers to erase the evidence in a surprisingly short time.

The accommodation *bashas* were constructed on the sand in a wide arc around one larger hut which was the cookhouse. In this hut one's plate and mug were simply filled by the cooks, then it was necessary to cross a kind of yard to eat at rough tables beneath an atap shaded area. One could always spot someone new to the camp because he did not think to crouch over the plateful of food he was carrying. Failure to take this precaution meant that the holder was wide open to aerial attack from kites, colloquially referred to by airmen as shitehawks, which would perch expectantly on the cookhouse roof awaiting any unsuspecting airman walking across the yard in an upright position. Many reached the tables with their faces literally covered in egg, much to the merriment of those already consuming their grub.

Anything unconsumed was not left lying around for long as it would soon receive the attention of some predator or other. Vultures were never far away and could usually be seen wheeling around languidly in the sky waiting to drop in on a target area where a meal might be found. No doubt they had been well fed in recent years by the comings and goings of the warring nations. At mealtimes they would often alight close to the cookhouse, their cold beady eyes, atop their pink scrawny necks, always on the lookout for anything animal that was not moving. Often they would gorge themselves on offal thrown out by the cooks, to the extent that they had great difficulty taking to the air again. Basically, they were cowardly creatures, and seemed only too aware they were unloved by all and sundry; but their scavenging served a useful purpose, and they always kept a respectful distance from live human beings.

A smaller, earthbound scavenger that came out at night and would patrol the billets in search of scraps, was a large variety of toad. Anything dropped on the floor was likely to be consumed by them, even the stubs of cigarettes!

We had only been at Cox's Bazar for a short while when the corporal airframe fitter on A flight was posted back to India. It had never occurred to me that I might be the most senior LAC fitter on the unit until I reached the billet at the end of a working day to find a pair of chevrons chalked on my kit box. Never having regarded myself very highly as a technician I had not expected to reach the dizzy heights of NCO. Somehow I had managed to keep my nose clean, and my pilot of 'F' for Freddy for the past two years, 'Charles' Laughton, also recently promoted to Flt/Lt., might well have had something to do with my elevation. It was an unexpected pleasure to be sewing 'tapes' on my shirts and tunics in place of the single red propeller denoting the rank of leading aircraftsman. The extra cash might come in handy too.

Life at Cox's Bazar was really very pleasant, and looking back on it was probably the happiest time of my service career. 273 Squadron was the only unit stationed there although from time to time other aircraft would make use of the single metal runway. There was the regular daily flight in of the Dakota, nicknamed the meat waggon, bringing our supplies. The ubiquitous Dakota was the life blood of the whole 14th Army. In spite of its bulk it could land and take off in as short a runway as a Spitfire, and would plod on in its own unglamorous way for years.

What our runway could not hope to cope with was the American B29 bomber. These giant four-engined planes could be seen flying high above us from bases in India to bomb targets down south. One afternoon, as we sat in 'readiness' by our Spits, we were told to expect a B29 making an emergency landing. It had been crippled on a bombing run by another B29 that had carelessly unloaded its cargo from above, and two bombs had gone right through the port wing and fuselage of the plane at the lower altitude. Fortunately the bombs had missed the crew, and the plane could still be flown with difficulty, but it would be unable to reach base. The main snag was that one of the bombs had severed the hydraulic system. The main undercarriage wheels had been lowered by hand, but we could see that the nose wheel was still firmly in its casing as the crippled plane came towards us, the pilot trying to maintain its balance for as long as possible before the aircraft, with its four great propellers feathered for maximum braking, inevitably tipped on to its nose. With a horrible grinding of metal on metal this happened right opposite our dispersal tent. Luckily, no fire occurred as the crew hastily evacuated. Miraculously, no one was hurt.

On another occasion a crippled B27 came in without warning from the opposite direction. Without the assistance of its landing flaps it had no chance of pulling up on the runway and ploughed into the sand at the southern end for nearly a quarter of a mile before finally coming to a halt.

Life on the Flights was really quite pleasant at Cox's. I could not help thinking how lucky our squadron was to be on the Arakan front, within a stone's throw of the sea, rather than sweating in some jungle clearing to the north of Assam. Daily routines were not too arduous, for we were not equipped for night flying, so the morning shift of the ground crews started around 7 a.m., after an early breakfast, who were then relieved at midday for tiffin, to return again for the late afternoon shift attending to the planes that had been on sweeps behind enemy lines. All the planes would be put to bed at sundown in dispersal bays just clear of the runway.

About once a week guard duties came around. This meant that six men, including the NCO in charge, would collect rations from the cookhouse at sunset before proceeding to the dispersal tent to relieve the ground crews of the afternoon shift.

Within days of being promoted to corporal I was detailed to take charge of the guard. The two men carrying out the last guard shift before dawn would wake up the other four men before first light, and the fitters, whether engine or airframe, would warm up the six Spits ready for 'stand by' duties or dawn patrol. Indeed, it was the only opportunity we airframe men ever got to start up a Spitfire.

Being unaccustomed to taking charge of things I was halfway down to the dispersal in the truck before one of the other five reminded me that we had not collected our rations from the cookhouse. It turned out to be a very lucky oversight otherwise we would just have been unloading by the airstrip when a Japanese sneak raider swooped in and deposited a stick of bombs amongst the parked aircraft.

I was actually gathering up our rations in the cookhouse when there was a shouted warning from the radio hut across the runway, followed by the manually operated klaxon which served as an air raid warning. Indeed, the bandit had already lined up his bomb drop before the klaxon sounded, and the nearby ack-ack battery was not able to swing into action until the raider was pulling up after his bombing run. Needless to say he got clean away as we made haste to get to the dispersal point to see what damage had been done.

Luckily, no one was hurt as the afternoon shift had already returned to their billet, and none of the planes had received a direct hit. Bits of shrapnel had struck four of them, so far as we could see by torchlight, and only one was sufficiently damaged to need repairs in the morning. At least it served as a reminder to us that we were still at war and the enemy was not so far away.

Our pilots needed no such reminding for they were frequently briefed to carry out sorties ahead of the advancing 14th Army. The targets were usually rivercraft or road convoys, although since the Japanese no longer controlled the skies movements of supplies were being restricted mainly to night time. The few railroads in Burma had been subjected to such heavy and prolonged batterings by the RAF that they were virtually no longer usable by the enemy.

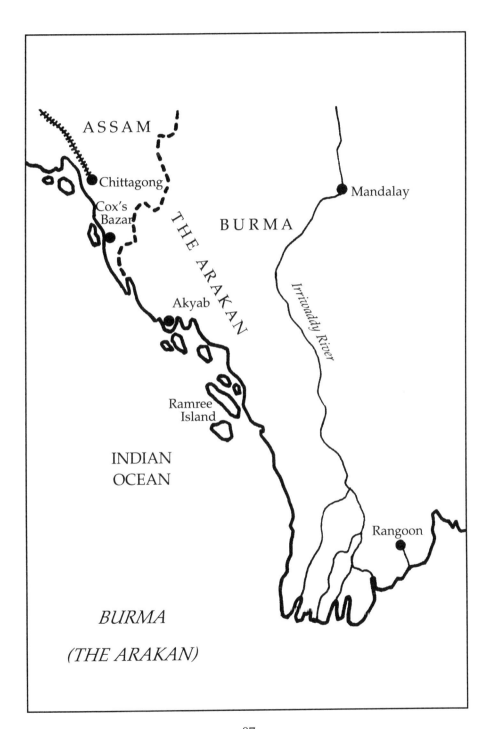

ASSAM

Chittagong

Cox's
Bazar

THE ARAKAN

BURMA

Mandalay

Irriwaddy River

Akyab

Ramree
Island

INDIAN
OCEAN

Rangoon

BURMA

(THE ARAKAN)

Chapter 14

My right hand man was an LAC who had been trained at Halton, the No. 1 technical training school near Wendover in Buckinghamshire. As such he clearly reckoned he knew more about aircraft than me; and he was probably right. I had been trained for just four months at the No. 6, wartime only, technical training school at Hednesford, Staffordshire, and later on a two-month conversion course at Innsworth Lane, Cheltenham.

Sandy Shaw and I became good friends and planned to take a leave together. By November I was entitled to take a couple of weeks' leave, and I had rather wanted to go 'up country' to the hill station at Darjeeling. The chance of travelling on the narrow gauge railway that wound its way up the Himalayan foothills rather appealed to me, not to mention the chance of glimpsing Mount Everest.

However, Sandy had a brother in the army who had been serving with Orde Wingate's Chindits behind the enemy lines, and Sandy had not heard from him for months until he got word that Eddie had survived the expedition but had been stricken with malaria and sent to convalesce in Bangalore. At short notice I agreed to accompany Sandy in an attempt to get to Bangalore. It meant turning left at Calcutta instead of right.

I had often hitch-hiked on the roads in England, and even in Ceylon, but had never attempted it by air. The first leg, to Dum Dum in Calcutta, was easy, for the 'meat waggon' flew in daily with supplies and returned to base empty. No trouble there to hop aboard the battered old Dakota, still reeking of the cargo it had carried in that morning. It was hardly the height of comfort for there was no seating in the hold, and as we headed out across the Bay of Bengal we ran into a violent thunderstorm. As we were tossed around we began to appreciate what it must often be like for our pilots as they searched the valleys of Burma for targets in monsoon conditions.

However, we did emerge from the blackness on the northern side and soon touched down at Dum Dum.

Whilst so close to the big city we decided to spend a couple of nights at a Services' club in town. As we were driven into the city on the back of a 15cwt RAF truck it was apparent that the famine that had stricken the delta area was not over, for dead and dying could still be counted alongside the road.

Calcutta is a place of great contrasts. That evening we visited the cinema. I can't remember anything about the film but the cinema was massive, luxuriously comfortable and air conditioned. Everything contrasted so greatly with the starving population just down the road. Next day we visited the beautifully tended central park where an Indian cricket eleven was engaged in an unofficial test match with a British Services team. Amongst those playing were two of my idols, Joe Hardstaff and Denis Compton who were then in their prime. I was to see the latter again a few weeks later, back at Cox's Bazar, when he was turning out for an England football eleven.

The following day Sandy and I returned to the airfield at Dum Dum to try to find a plane going to Bangalore. Planes of many types were scattered around the large perimeter. Our enquiries soon led us to a Dakota being refuelled and loaded up.

'We're due off at three o'clock in the morning,' said the pilot cheerily. 'You're welcome to jump aboard if you can find yourselves a space between all the gear in there.' That seemed a small discomfort on a flight that would take several hours.

The discomfort that we had not bargained for was the extreme cold as the plane climbed steadily above ten thousand feet. With no heating in the cargo hold, and clad only in khaki drill shirts and shorts we were frozen rigid. As the sun began to rise in the sky we touched down at some airfield near the East coast of India. When the cargo doors were opened a blast of hot air rushed in, and as we both staggered out to straighten our frozen joints it was like stepping into an oven. By mid-morning we reached Bangalore where it was still hot, being that much further south, but at 5,000 feet above sea level the air was not so oppressive. In spite of its altitude I was disappointed to find the terrain was rather flat and uninteresting.

Our first objective was to find somewhere to stay before Sandy sought out his brother in the Army convalescent camp.

The suburbs of Bangalore contained some quite elegant properties, some of which had been occupied by Europeans returning home because of the war. One such bore the sign Hotel outside which we decided would suit our purposes for a few nights. We were not deterred at being informed that the main building was fully occupied, but that we could, if we wished, have the outbuilding in the garden. We had no qualms about that; after all, Mary and Joseph had kipped down in a stable, and neither of us was pregnant! Indeed, we had slept in far worse places over the past four years.

Sandy had little trouble locating his brother Eddie, fair skinned and sandy haired also, but looking more than two years the senior, presumably because of his experiences in the Chindits with whom he had spent nine months behind enemy lines living off the land, apart from occasional supply drops from the RAF when they could be found. They had carried out many acts of sabotage to Japanese lines of communication which must have been a constant irritation to the enemy. However, hardships accentuated by the constant tension had taken toll of the health of Wingate's men and Eddie had been airlifted out with a high fever. Anyhow, there were little signs of that now and he was due to be released from convalescence in a couple of days or so.

Needless to say we three downed several pints in the Services' canteen as we exchanged yarns. These became more slurred as time went by; so much so that it was with some difficulty that we made our way back that afternoon to our hotel annex, collapsing on to our beds in a drunken stupor.

I awoke as the sun was setting, to the realisation that we were not alone in our outbuilding, which had probably been a stable in days gone by. The whirring of wings that greeted my ears was not generated by angels but by little furry things passing overhead as they flew from one corner of the ceiling to another. I had never been in close proximity to bats before and had thought of them as something to be avoided. There was no chance of that here, so the best thing seemed to be to make friends with them, for we were unlikely to be able to shoo them out. After all, it was their home. I can recall, on catching one, my surprise on finding how rodent-like it was: a fair description would be an airborne mouse. A few crumbs of Kitkat, scraped from the corners of my sidepack, and we were friends for life.

In fact, we did not stay in Bangalore for a whole week as there was not much reason to stay after Sandy had bid farewell to brother Eddie when he returned to his unit. For one thing we had made no plans about how we should get back to Cox's Bazar. Frankly, Bangalore did not match up to my expectations. I would rather have been sampling the cool mountain breezes of Darjeeling.

We watched a football match that was heralded as England v. Italy, played on an arena that bore not a single blade of grass. The Italians were prisoners of war who had been herded behind barbed wire since the early days of General Wavell's advances in Libya. What they had lacked in the skills of war they certainly made up for with a football, leaving our scratch Services team flatfooted as they piled in the goals.

Getting back to Dum Dum was not as easy as we had expected. We had to persuade a transport officer at the airport that we were urgently needed by our squadron, and then we had to wait a couple of days before we could be squeezed into the hold of a Dakota.

It was on the flight that Sandy began to show signs of succumbing to illness. His usually florid features were taking on a greying look, and black rings began to show beneath reddening orbs. There was little doubt he was sickening with a fever.

It was when we moved up to India that we were first introduced to the mepachrine tablet. It was a little yellow pill that was prescribed for every man to take each day. It was certainly effective against malaria, in spite of generating the yellowing features of a Mongolian, and provided it was consumed regularly it would prevent the dreaded fever breaking out.

Of course, in our haste to get away we had forgotten to arm ourselves with fourteen days supply of tablets from the sick bay. Clearly, Sandy was beginning to pay the price. As I had spent three and a half years out east being pierced regularly by the proboscises of mosquitos I had come to believe that I was immune from malaria. Wishful thinking.

At Dum Dum it was not possible to air hitch back to Cox's because the daily 'meat waggon' Dakota was filled to capacity with cargo. So it meant that we would have to return to base from Calcutta in the manner the squadron had moved initially; by train to the Bramaputra, then the long ferry journey downstream to board another train to Chittagong, and then the coastal steamer back to Cox's Bazar During all of the two days that it took, Sandy was getting steadily worse. I was having to carry his gear for he was barely able to support himself. What was more, I was beginning to feel groggy myself.

Somehow we managed to reach camp where Sandy was taken straight into hospital. I reported sick and was admitted too.

Chapter 15

My bout of malaria was quite mild, so I was released from hospital ahead of Sandy. Life had been progressing on 273 Squadron much the same during the two weeks in November we had been away from Cox's. The weather was hot and dry, which meant that the nearby stream, where we used to bathe at sunset, had now dried up. As a result we either had to walk the half mile to the seashore for a salt water bath or dig down in the sand for fresh water. Gradually the hollow near each *basha* became deeper and deeper, and by Christmas water had become a precious commodity.

Our pilots were still carrying out sweeps inland to the east, ahead of the steadily advancing 14th Army, or to the south around Akyab. Rumours were rife that 273 would soon be moving south also, to an airstrip in Burma proper.

As another Christmas approached, my fourth and probably last overseas, there was a happy atmosphere in the camp. News from Europe was encouraging and the Nazi regime looked to be entering its death throes. However, the stubbornness of the Japanese might mean that the war on our front would continue yet for quite a while.

In our small corner of the global conflict Christmas was a time for relaxing as much as possible and eating and drinking. The cooks excelled themselves by producing a terrific feast in the decorated dining hall. Rationing went by the board for two days as we were granted the privilege of helping ourselves, whilst beer flowed freely.

About this time there was a new directive from the upper strata of the Air Force which would directly affect the ground crews. It meant that the pilots need not be restricted to returning to their home bases if it became expedient to touch down for refuelling and servicing elsewhere after sorties. We were to be designated number 7273 Echelon, and as such we would be expected to attend to the needs of aircraft other than those of 273 Squadron.

Technically, this reorganisation was sound, as the move southwards towards the eventual goal of Singapore progressed. On the other hand a bond had developed between pilots and ground crews, with the latter taking a pride in 'their kite', while the former were always relieved, when returning from sorties, to see their fitter waving them in to the dispersal point. It was regrettable that the new set-up would surely affect the *esprit de corps* of the squadron. That was a very real asset with a comparatively small band of men working together with one aim, the victorious completion of the war. It was a long and tested tradition of the Royal Air Force that was being threatened. The new system was to be put to the test soon after Christmas when the main party of 273 were ordered to move forward to a temporary airstrip on dried out paddy fields just across the border into Burma. It was on New Year's Eve that we moved forward in lorry convoy to set up camp at Maunghnama. This was virgin territory for the RAF; there was no metal strip runway, just the hardened earth of the erstwhile paddy fields over which both Allied and Japanese armies had advanced and retreated over the past three years.

Our inclination, on arrival, was to set up our tents, for that was how we were to sleep at Maunghnama. Strangely enough I had never slept in a tent in all of my life. However, our twelve planes had landed and our priority was to disperse them off the landing strip for the night and carry out inspections ready for operations to begin the next day. Tool boxes were dumped from the lorry carrying equipment, and a tent was erected nearby to serve as the flight dispersal HQ. These jobs accomplished, we could then turn our attention to the living area which consisted of a clearing in the scrub that had served the Army as a cemetery. Our tents had been pegged out to take six men to each tent. I did not fancy sleeping on the ground, so I managed to find sufficient pieces of timber to rig up a makeshift bed with my groundsheet suspended a few inches above the soil.

This proved to be fortuitous in the light of a fierce tropical storm that broke during the night, flooding several of the tents. Being a heavy sleeper I was not even aware that others had been drenched in the small hours when their tents collapsed and rainwater flooded in.

It was still raining when dawn broke, and first light revealed a miserable sight as rivulets flowed between, and even through, the tents. When we reached the landing strip it had turned into a lake, with the landing wheels of the Spits half submerged. So much for the operational sweep planned for that day. Indeed,

93

there was nothing we could hope to do for at least a couple of days, or until the flood subsided sufficiently for take off to be attempted.

The cooks, who had probably served as boy scouts in their time, produced quite a feast, albeit mostly with tinned food. At least the rain had provided plentiful washing facilities.

It was here that I met up with an effervescent character in our flight tent nicknamed Rubberdick Roy. He was a married man, small of build, with an ever cheerful disposition who had not long since left behind in Blighty a young wife and a new born baby daughter. To prove it he carried with him a tiny pair of bootees, which he suspended above his bed space.

After his evening shower it was evident how he acquired his nickname: his penis appeared to be made of elastic! He pulled it out to dry it to a length that brought tears to one's eyes. At full stretch he would release his foreskin and everything would practically disappear in a shower of talcum powder. It seemed unbelievable that his paraphernalia worked properly, but the bootees gave proof that it had. Also, he was always cheerful.

The storm gave us an enforced forty-eight hour leave while the landing strip dried out and the squadron awaited fresh instructions. With no recreational facilities available a small party of us set out to scale a nearby promontory to take stock of our whereabouts. It was quite a climb through the undergrowth which led on top to a series of slit trenches which presumably had not long since been evacuated by the Japanese. It would not have surprised us to find a few decomposed corpses, but all had been cleared up.

On the third day at Maunghnama the signal came through for us to return, not to Cox's Bazar but to Chittagong.

Events had been moving fast on the Burma front and it had been decided at Mountbatten's headquarters that now was the time to move towards the capture of Akyab, and beyond that Rangoon. To do so meant moving air cover closer to the action. To hope to achieve this 273 Squadron were detailed to set up home on the offshore island of Ramree which was still partially in enemy hands.

To accomplish this bold plan the ground personnel would be put ashore by landing craft of the sort used some seven months earlier on the beaches of Normandy. This required re-equipping with water-proofed vehicles, not to mention new green drill for personnel, presumably so that we would not show up too clearly for Jap snipers to pot at. To the amusement of all, part of our new rig-out included three condoms, known then as french letters. These were intended to seal up one's wristwatch and any other small articles of value that might be impaired by contact with sea water. There seemed little chance that they might be used for their manufactured purpose!

I was one of a party who volunteered to collect from a transport dump the waterproofed vehicles that we would need to transfer men and equipment, including water and fuel, from landing barges on to the beach at Ramree. All the 'gharries' were fitted with air intake pipes venting some six feet above ground level. There was little doubt we were going to get our feet wet.

Ramree Island, at its nearest point in the north, which was where we were to land and set up camp, was some three hundred miles south of Chittagong, extending a further fifty miles southwards and tapering into marshes close to the mainland just to the north of the small Burmese port of Taungup. The area at the start of 1945 was still occupied by the Japanese, but their depleted, and probably demoralised, forces were being driven from the north of the island by the Army, which should enable the squadron to operate from close to a small port named Kyaukpyu.

At this time I was only two months short of serving the stipulated four years abroad (for single men), and I expect that I could have opted out of the hardships ahead. Once committed to the invasion force there would probably be no chance of returning to Blighty until hostilities reached their final conclusions, whenever that might be.

My feelings were mixed. Much as I would like to be in England again, with my family and steady pen friend Doris, I had been involved in the Far Eastern war since its very first day on 7 December 1941 when Jap bombs rained unexpectedly down upon us as we set off through the rubber trees of northern Malaya to have breakfast.

Deep within me I knew that I wanted to be in at the kill, perhaps even to march in a victory parade in Singapore. Then there was the basic love of excitement and the sharing of troubles with comrades as we coped with unknown problems ahead. All of these things I would miss if I pressed to be released for repatriation. So I kept quiet and packed my kitbag once again; not forgetting the condoms.

It was on 21 January, just one week after my twenty-fifth birthday, that I joined my mates aboard the lorry that took us down to the jetty to board the boat for Ramree.

Chapter 16

The vessel was a good deal larger than the coastal boat we had used a couple of times to reach Cox's Bazar. For the couple of nights aboard we were issued with hammocks, the first time I had slept that way since March 1941 aboard the old *Warwick Castle*, since confined to Davy's Locker by German torpedoes. Our main concern, certainly uppermost in my mind, was what sort of reception we might expect when ordered to wade ashore on Ramree Island.

Under cover of darkness the ship anchored offshore in the bay. When we had embarked we had been ordered to remain as quiet as possible at all times. No one needed reminding of that as we stood on deck with our packs on our backs and grasping our kitbags, having tucked our watches in our top pockets, each safe in its condom.

It seemed an age before an army officer ordered us to scramble down the nets covering the vessel's sides and into the waiting barges, which pulled away for the shore as soon as they were full. The final gaining of terra firma involved little more of a wetting than paddling at low tide off Southend.

There was little for us to do but wait in a sheltered part of the beach where we had been herded whilst our transport was unloaded and marshalled on dry land. After the hubbub of the landing all became quiet again as the empty landing craft returned to the mother ship. Thankfully, there was no sound of gunfire either, although we were told that the first assault wave at dawn, under cover of naval bombardment, had met with stiff opposition, but the Japanese had now retreated towards the centre and south of the island.

By high noon we were moved in lorries to a small airstrip alongside the village of Kyaukpyu. A partially destroyed Buddhist pagoda gave evidence that warfare had passed that way.

Our first task was to get the airstrip, which was originally a dry stretch of sandy grassland some eighty yards long, ready to receive our Spits. For the pilots this was a very short landing strip, but all touched down safely on the first occasion. However, on subsequent familiarisation flights no fewer than three pranged on touchdown, damaging airscrews and nose cowlings. The laying of metal strips a few days later, as at Cox's Bazar, made things a little easier, but still the strip was too short for the comfort of the pilots, who also had to contend with trees close at one end. It was not until some weeks later that work began to lengthen the runway.

For the ground crews, who managed to rig up a crude shelter close to the airstrip, life at first at Kyaukpyu was particularly uncomfortable, and being a few degrees nearer to the equator the heat at midday was overbearing. Within a couple of days we took delivery of tents, and life became a little more bearable, in spite of the intense heat on the airstrip which was accentuated when the metal strips were laid down. At least the sea was near at hand to cool down in when possible.

However, there was little time for recreation for now was the time for the squadron, now in the most advanced position in Burma, to make its presence felt by the enemy. Six planes were kept in readiness throughout the daylight hours. For the pilots it meant sitting around in full flying kit, whilst the fitters would shelter as much as possible from the sun beneath the Spitfire's wings.

Many of the squadron's operations were in support of ground troops on the mainland, and by reports they were highly successful. By now the pilots were extremely experienced at ground attacks with 20mm cannons and guns, and their close support sorties were often within one hundred yards of the 14th Army troops as they moved rapidly southwards.

Around this time the squadron was equipped with 500lb bombs, which arrived with instructions from the UK where Spitfires had been bombing V1 buzz bombs launching sites in Northern France. Their technique was to fly above the target at about eight thousand feet, still in formation, with the leader targeting through his gunsights, then all would let their bombs go at once. When this technique was practised over the airfield it was not too successful. The high mountains and monsoon rain clouds rendered it impracticable. The pilots decided to ignore instructions from the UK, instead using delay fuses in the bombs and dropping them at low level. With practice this method became increasingly successful

The danger with low level attacks was, of course, the risk of not pulling up in time, and two of our pilots were lost in the hazardous terrain of the Tungupe Prome road. In addition, there were two pilots that had been killed during the few days at Maunghnama. In all, no fewer than fourteen pilots were killed in accidents during my time on 273 Squadron.

Usually, pilots took off soon after dawn in pairs to seek out targets. Because the Japs usually moved their supplies at night time, since the RAF had control of the skies, most vehicles and supply dumps were camouflaged during the day with foliage. Two young pilots, during afternoon sweeps, noticed that these could often be detected because the heat of the midday sun had wilted the leaves. This discovery led to a much greater success rate.

Lord Mountbatten, himself young by comparison with other supreme commanders, had begun to gather around him younger men to carry out his ambitious plans to end the Burma campaign. One such was the Earl of Brandon, recently promoted to Air Vice Marshal, who had survived the Battle of Britain and who lived in the traditional gung-ho style of fighter pilots. As AOC 224 Group, of which we were part, he wanted to see for himself how Spitfires operated in a forward area.

Usually he arrived in his Harvard, wearing the briefest of shorts, even after a Standing Order that all pilots should wear trousers at all times. Often he would fly on sorties, commandeering one of the Spits and discarding his badges of high rank to fly as a humble Flying Officer. He was well loved by all who met up with him.

By February we had settled down well; literally, concerning the tents which were pitched on sand. Digging down a couple of feet or so served dual purposes: it was much easier moving around inside the tent, and it would give some protection against anti-personnel bombs should Jappo consider a sneak raid.

Had it rained heavily we would probably have been flooded, but the next monsoon was not due for some while and we could expect to move again before then. For now the days were dry and the sun beat mercilessly down. Luckily, the evenings were quite cool, at least by comparison, and that was when we did our digging. As at Cox's Bazar fresh water could be found by excavation, and when the water table from the last monsoon was reached enough water would seep into the holes throughout the working day to provide a reasonable wash down at nightfall. As the weeks passed by the holes got larger, and by the time we moved on had sunk from the surface by some fifteen feet.

Rations were mostly of the tinned variety, with corned beef and Maconocies, as always, to the fore. Luckily, I would eat anything that was dished up, and the cooks did do their best with what they had.

Some local produce became available, and one enterprising Burmese visited the camp offering chickens for sale. One or two of the lads built pens to keep the hens for egg laying, which provided a welcome supplement. When the time came to move they finally surrendered themselves to a chicken stew.

The armourers, in their tent, were less fortunate with their poultry enterprise when two birds for which they had bartered became airborne and flew off into the branches of a nearby cashew tree!

The cashew tree itself was a useful source of nutriment. When the runway began to be extended we were obliged to move our tents to make room for the operation, but we were pleasantly surprised to be able to relocate near to a cashew tree which not only provided shade but also fruit. Most of us were familiar with the nuts but not the fruit that surrounded them, which was very palatable. On the debit side the trees also provided the staple diet of the fruit bats which would descend at night creating quite a commotion, as well as the problem of their droppings.

The recognised currency on Ramree was the bush shirt. One shirt would buy six small egg-laying chickens. The going rate for labour was one shirt per day, which was a good bargain when a man could put up half a dozen charpoys in a day.

One of our number, with religious inclinations, even employed six men to erect a small bamboo church at a cost of twelve shirts. For that he had received the CO's approval, so the shirts were provided from stores.

In general, it was a carefree existence for airmen, although rifles and tin helmets needed to be carried at all times. There was no local entertainment, but from time to time well-known showbiz personalities came our way and all were well received. Names that come to mind are Patricia Burke, and a week later, her mother Marie. George Formby also gave a show which did much to relieve the daily monotony of our work, and the boredom of evenings spent in the tents with rather primitive lighting

Many evenings were spent simply writing to our folk back home, or reading. One local source of literature was the Far East Forces newspaper whose official reporter, Nevile Shute, later became a world famous author. Unbeknown to us at the time he paid a visit to Kyaukpyu, painting a very vivid picture of life on the camp for the next publication of the newspaper.

Leisure-time thoughts of most red blooded RAF men was not to be satisfied however. A group of airmen out walking in the local village were reported to have seen ahead of them a bevy of shapely bare-topped girls. Once past them they turned round to get a better view only to be slightly disenchanted by the large cigars stuck into the girls' mouths. Cigars or not they were happy to fraternise, but the villagers were soon moved well away from the airstrip.

By the end of March it became apparent that we would be moving again soon. Targets within range of our Spitfires were now becoming scarcer as the Japs retreated, and the airstrip, which had by now been lengthened by a thousand yards, would be left for the longer ranged squadron of Thunderbolts which had just moved in to reinforce the aerial offensive. Even having lengthened the runway it was still barely enough for heavily laden Thunderbolts to get off the ground, and many a heart was in one's mouth as these aircraft struggled to get off the ground. Although none of the Thunderbolts failed to get airborne there was one that returned from a sortie on fire and crashed on landing, killing the pilot.

Regrettably, two of our pilots were lost around this time, Smithers and Stan Crowe. Both went down attacking enemy targets on the Irrawaddy river.

One morning in mid April I was detailed, with a group of airmen, to report with my kit in order to form the advance party for the next move. The following day our party boarded transport which moved us to another part of the island where several tents were already erected. We were then paraded to be told that we would soon be going to Elephant Point, just down river from Rangoon, some four hundred miles from where we stood. It was clear that the High Command was poised for the kill by the capture of Rangoon itself, thereby virtually ending the war in Burma.

On Ramree island there were still some Japanese remaining. They had been driven southwards from the centre of the island leaving behind intricate fortifications from which it was evident they had lived in squalor, judging by the stench and rancid litter lying around.

Hungry and dejected, the surviving Japs had retreated southwards and into the swampy ground nearest to the Burmese mainland where they may have hoped to find small craft to ferry them across the water. It would never occur to them to surrender. But there were no boats, only crocodiles who could not believe their luck. It led to the greatest orgy of human flesh eating by beasts ever recorded.

For several days we awaited the summons to embark on the naval ships, as we had done at Chittagong. In the meantime, the camp was close to the sea, so we spent most of our time bathing in the heavy seas which had been whipped up by the approaching spring monsoon. At least we were keeping fit battling in the surging surf which would have provided ideal surfing conditions had we any boards handy.

At last came the order to board ship. Once again we were issued with three condoms and iron rations as we prepared for whatever lay ahead.

Chapter 17

Our naval ship, with its landing barges in the open hold astern, eased out into the Bay of Bengal heading due south for some two hundred miles before veering east to round the delta of the Irrawaddy, then north-easterly to Elephant Point at the entrance of the Rangoon River. Here the ship anchored and we were ordered over the side, again clambering down the nets into the landing barges drawn up alongside.

The skies had been leaden throughout our journey, choosing this moment to unleash their watery burden. The monsoon had started in earnest, and, judging by the stair-rods, looked like lasting quite a while. The landing barges chugged to the shore, which was black, flat and forbidding, made worse by the rain. The landing ramps were lowered and our small advance party advanced into oily black water, with thick sticky mud sucking at our feet. We were soaked through before reaching the top of the bank. Had the Japs been waiting for us we could not have cared less; but there was no sign or sound of any Japanese – perhaps it was just too wet for them.

The whole landscape was black and uninviting, with paddy fields stretching away to the horizon and rapidly becoming a sea of mud.

Groups of soldiers and airmen began to form up while we awaited instructions. It was suggested that we partook of some of our rations, but hunger was not our main priority. From somewhere a weak brew of tea was produced. It did little to relieve the misery of our situation.

After a while the Army moved off and we were left to make our own way to slightly higher ground some two fields away. It was here that we had been expected to prepare a landing strip, but we were now informed that it would no longer be necessary as the Japanese had abandoned Mingladon, the airfield for Rangoon. It would, in any case, have been impossible for aircraft to land under present conditions. There was no denying the forces of the elements. We

102

were told that next day we would be going up river into the city, and to reclaim the old RAF camp at Mingladon, but in the meantime we would just have to kip down for the night.

Still the rain tippled incessantly as we consumed the remainder of our emergency rations, and then tried to settle for the night with only our capes for cover. We had been told not to make any noise or strike a light in case the enemy might still be around. Evidently the same instructions had not been given to a corps of Indian Pioneers, settling in on the next field, who lit a huge bonfire, amid shouting and banging that would have aroused even a dead Japanese.

The night was one of the longest, wettest and most uncomfortable of my life, and dawn seemed an age arriving. First light revealed the desolation all around. The stair-rods had subsided to a steady drizzle which never looked like ending. Our rations were gone too.

In the nadir of our despair we heard the drone of aircraft approaching. Surely they could not be enemy planes.

As they came in low through the clouds we could identify Dakotas, and on closer inspection the hatches were open for a supply drop. It was manna from heaven as we watched the parachutes open, and we lost no time in retrieving the canisters. In some were tins of self heating drinks, the likes of which I had not seen before, or since. A small cap in the centre of a cylinder could be prised off revealing a wick, which, when lit, burnt for about a minute, enough to provide a very welcome hot drink. There were several varieties such as Bovril, Ovaltine and cocoa, not to mention various soups. With the liquids came American 'K' rations, despised by the Yanks but enjoyed by us, particularly under the circumstances. Indeed, anything would have been appreciated at that time.

As the day wore on, so did the rain continue, and it looked as if we would be spending another miserable night on the mud flats while we awaited orders that were not forthcoming. Some were beginning to improvise crude shelters, using bushes and groundsheets, when a naval barge pulled in to the bank and a friendly voice hailed us.

'Does anyone want a lift to Rangoon?'

We obtained official sanction and our group were helped aboard and told by the skipper to strip off our sodden clothing and they would dry them for us. Blankets were lent to drape around us. This was hospitality indeed.

I went up on deck as the vessel pulled out into mid stream. The scene of the previous night and day, and the misery it had brought, faded in the dusk to our stern as we headed north upstream.

'I wouldn't swap your job for mine,' volunteered one of the matelots.

'This has been an exception rather than the rule,' I replied.

'Nevertheless, I feel safer at sea,' he responded.

I felt dubious about his statement when we heard explosions ahead of us, learning later that one barge had been sunk and another badly damaged by mines that had been planted by the British Navy during the evacuation of Rangoon in 1942. Fortunately we got through unscathed and were able to tie up against the quay in Rangoon.

Although by now our clothes had dried out we were offered the hospitality of another night on board, and gladly accepted. The Navy has always been closer to the RAF than the Army, and we were full of gratitude for all they had done for us, not to mention the hearty breakfast before we set out to find somewhere to sleep the following night.

I went up on deck, where the rain had stopped at last, and gazed across the river as the swollen brown water raced by. In my mind's eye I saw again, as if in slow motion, the good ship *Hang Tau*, which had carried me and my two mates Brem and Fruity all the way from Japanese-occupied Penang, together with the three Chinese daughters of the skipper, only to fall victim to Jap dive bombers. A lump came to my throat as I remembered the blissful moments spent with the lovely Tau Fong during and before that fateful journey. Tears welled up as I thought of her lissome body being swept away downstream.

'Wakey wakey, Ken,' I heard someone call, 'aren't you coming for a stroll in town?'

Gathering up my kit I returned to the present and joined the others on the quayside as we waved our naval friends farewell and set off towards the city.

It was an eerie sensation walking through deserted streets, with shops shuttered or boarded up. Everywhere there was filth, and a smell of burning pervaded over all. The enemy had left in a hurry without bothering to tidy up!

We hoped that they had not had any time to set any booby traps, and were constantly on our guard. At last we came upon a school, empty and completely devoid of furniture. It would suit us as a temporary residence while we awaited orders to move in to Mingladon.

Using timber from bombed buildings we soon had a fire going to dry out our blankets, still wet from the night at Elephant Point. It enabled us also to prepare a makeshift meal with what rations we had left. It reminded me of the days spent in a school in Batavia in February 1942 when we were refugees on the run. Then there was still plenty of food in the shops, and even entertainment in the city, but most were too ill after escaping from Sumatra to be able to eat and enjoy themselves. Here it was just the opposite: we were physically fit, but there was nothing to be bought or enjoyed in Rangoon in that first week of May 1945.

Whilst we had been making our way from Ramree we were oblivious to the fact that the final drama of the defeat of the German Third Reich was being played out, and Hitler's charred body, together with that of his recently married mistress Eva Braun, lay in the Reichstag garden in Berlin. Celebrations for the victory in Europe had been fixed for 8 May. This fact was little comfort to us, five thousand miles away and behind enemy lines, with the end of the war not yet in sight. The re-occupation of the capital of Burma should have made headline news in England, but was probably pushed to one corner in deference to events much nearer to home. It made us feel very much the forgotten Air Force in the forgotten Army.

Everywhere in Rangoon there was filth and degradation; even the cathedral had been defiled, having been used by the Japs as a storehouse and for the stabling of mules. In many streets we found piles of occupation money, now completely worthless.

On returning to our temporary home we were glad to be told that we would be moving the next day, 5 May, to Mingladon, the airfield a few miles from Rangoon. It had been a peacetime station of the RAF, with brick buildings, and so we expected to find decent billets. We were not disappointed.

We were the first to move in, so the choice of living space was ours, although there were no beds or water supply. As expected, the latrines were in a filthy state, but at least the wash basins were still there for when water could be found, although the desire for showers would have to wait.

By now we were quite proficient at improvisation. Primitive charpoys were constructed out of metal piping, cross laced with electric flex, enough to support a groundsheet above the level of the concrete floor.

Our immediate priority was to prepare the airfield to receive our Spits. The runways had been badly cratered by Allied bombers, so that landing was not going to be easy. Until heavy earthmoving equipment was available we could not carry out more than a temporary repair job on the runway, apart from marking out the danger spots.

It was on 7 May that I heard the unmistakable drone of a Spitfire approaching. It circled a couple of times to line up our crude markings before touching down perfectly and taxiing its way, carefully avoiding craters, to the damaged hangars.

The pilot slid back his cockpit roof, announcing that the war in Europe had ceased two days previously. We were so out of touch with fast moving world events that it was like being on another planet.

Soon, the remainder of 273 Squadron followed in, and once again we were an operational unit, fighting two hundred miles behind enemy lines to the north.

It was just as well that the Spits had been able to land at Mingladon, for they were well past the point of no return from Ramree, as there was no other liberated landing ground within range. It was a daring move by the Group Command, but one that paid off.

It was not long before normality began to return as equipment was flown in and repairs undertaken. Water was laid on to the ablutions, so once again we could indulge in the luxury of a shower. Generators were installed to provide electricity, and even a cinema was rigged up on the verandah of the dining hall.

Newsreels were shown of the horrors of Belsen and other concentration camps in Europe. We began to wonder what horrors awaited us when hostilities eventually ended in our part of the world. What had happened to those mates of mine from 27 Squadron who had not been so lucky in Malaya and the Dutch East Indies? Where were all those servicemen trapped in Singapore? Could any have survived the known cruelties of the Japanese military regime to whom surrender was anathema? Time would tell.

Our main party had now arrived, and transport vehicles were moving in to give us our operational life blood. By mid-May our planes were patrolling defensively, just in case what was left of the Jap Air Force decided to launch a counter bombing offensive; but now it would seem that all their planes that had survived in Burma had now been moved to prop up the defences nearer to Japan.

One day whilst clearing out the hangars an extraordinary find was unearthed in one of the corners. It was a damaged wooden propeller off a pre-war light plane, and with the splintered tips there was a grubby brass plate. I wonder if any Japanese airmen knew who Amy Johnson was? She had used the airfield at Rangoon as a staging post on her record-breaking solo flight to Australia in 1935. Somehow it had been allowed to survive the years of occupation.

Soon after the victory in Europe came the dissolution of parliament in the UK, and the general election in which all servicemen, both home and abroad, could vote by proxy. I often wonder why so many of my mates looked towards the Left. It was said that it was the servicemen's votes that were responsible for the ousting of the government under Churchill who had guided the country to ultimate victory.

However, even after the election of Clement Atlee the war had not been won in the Far East. That was to come with dramatic suddenness in mid-August, just a few days after the catastrophic dropping of two atomic bombs over Hiroshima and Nagasaki by American Super Fortresses. We did not know then just how much those two bombs were going to change the world.

Chapter 18

In early August, just prior to the dropping of the two atomic bombs, High Command had given the green light for the implementation of 'Tiger Force', the name given by Mountbatten for the recapture of Singapore and the Malayan Peninsula. 7273 Echelon were ready to be part of this force. It was with some relief that we now knew we would no longer need our tin hats and all the equipment for a beach landing. The actual landing had been fixed for 28 August on beaches between Port Dickson and Malacca.

When the hostilities ceased I began to feel restless, as did several others. Surely there was no longer any need for us to be hanging around Mingladon merely carrying out daily inspections on the Spitfires. There would doubtless be mopping up operations carried out in the Far East, but for me England called, and being the longest serving abroad of any of the squadron's personnel I considered that I was now due for repatriation. My application to the commanding officer was treated with sympathy and I was told to stand by.

Within a few days I was told that a Liberator would be landing the following day for re-fuelling prior to going on to Singapore, and I could be included amongst its passengers. At Seletar, on Singapore island, where the RAF was beginning to re-establish its headquarters, I could expect to be given a place aboard the first available troopship bound for Blighty.

The following morning I bade farewell to the dwindling band of airmen left on 273 Squadron, with whom I had served for three and a half years, and boarded the Liberator for the five-hour journey to Singapore. I was travelling in the opposite direction to the ultimate journey back to England which would add another four or five weeks, but at least I should be back in Blighty well before Christmas. It was now the first week in September.

In Singapore I was now on my own again, which was a situation I had not experienced for a long time. Men came and went throughout my time on 273

Squadron, but always there was someone to rely upon as a friend when comrades were posted to other units. Now I knew no one that I could call a friend; but Blighty and home were not too far away.

On reporting to headquarters at Seletar, which was still in a state of flux, I was told that it was not possible to get me on a troopship for a couple of weeks at least, because of the priority of repatriating the prisoners of war who had been released from Changi jail, and who were still assembling from other prisoner of war camps in the Far East. Those that I saw were mostly in a very sorry state, emaciated in the extreme, some having lost limbs. The medical orderlies were doing their best, with the help of many volunteers, to get the walking skeletons fit enough to face the journey home. It did not bear thinking about the numbers that we were told had perished during their three and a half years as prisoners of war. It was clear that the Japanese had no regard at all for the Geneva Conventions relating to war prisoners.

It was difficult to control one's resentment, to the point of revulsion, of our recent Oriental enemy when tales were related about the gangs of men forced to work on the construction of the Burma railway which the Japanese had constructed, with great loss of life, to link by rail Bangkok with Rangoon.

It became doubly difficult to contain one's anger when a party of some fifty Japanese were seen herded into a compound. They were little more than boys, recently sent from Japan as reinforcements, now awaiting orders from the Allied Command. They looked frightened, and probably had reason to be if not protected from some Allied servicemen who might well have taken the law into their hands on a dark night. One had to try to maintain a civilised attitude, but resentment would take a long time to die.

Having been allocated a bed space in one of the pre-war billets which had now been cleared out, my instructions were to report to the Orderly Room each day until a firm date for departure could be given to me. In the meantime, Lord Mountbatten was anxious to carry out a formal surrender ceremony at the City Hall, Singapore. It was to be held the following week, on 12 September, and any fit personnel who could be spared were to be marshalled for the event. I was detailed to be one of them.

I had not dressed up for a formal parade for a very long time, for there had been a complete absence of what was known as bullshit on active service squadrons. With Lord Mountbatten, who accepted the token sword of surrender from the most senior ranked Japanese, were the commanders of the three services, General Slim, Admiral Power, and Sir Keith Park representing the Royal Air Force.

The ceremony was staged for the world to witness the final humiliation of the Japanese military régime which had planned and instigated the war. To the Japanese the very act of surrendering was anathema, and several high ranking Japanese officers had already committed suicide.

For the likes of me, merely killing time before sailing for home, the actual ceremony was quite simply boring. I just could not work up enthusiasm for the fact that history was being made; or rather, being seen to be made. Also, it was a very hot and uncomfortable day for marching around and standing in front of the Singapore Town Hall.

Chapter 19

The following morning I reported once more to the Orderly Room to be told that I would be embarking the following week on 20 September, not by boat, as I had expected, but by air! So my journey down from Rangoon had been unnecessary as I would now be returning there for the first leg of the journey which would probably take three or four days over all. That was the bright side; at least I should be home about a month earlier than I would have been if going by boat.

The reason given for the change of plan was that the many hundreds of prisoners were not in a fit state to withstand the rigours of flight. The boat trip would be more relaxing, with better medical facilities, and give their gaunt frames more chance to resemble normality before their relatives saw them.

In the meantime I could take seven days' leave if I wished. Suddenly, I felt the desire to retrace my steps taken in May 1941 when first I was in Singapore to join 27 Squadron: a very new aircraftsman second class airframe fitter yet to put his skills to the test on a proper squadron, having only just passed out from training school before being sent overseas to a destination unknown.

On that occasion, seven months before the Japanese invasion of Malaya, and relishing peacetime conditions after the Battle of Britain and the London Blitz, our band of thirty replacements for 27 Squadron's old sweats travelled north by train. As always, I liked the idea of travelling by rail, but now the journey would be unreliable as the rail system had not yet been restored to peacetime conditions. Japanese maintenance during the occupation had been virtually non-existent, added to the fact that Allied bombers had scored a few hits in various places.

There was no difficulty hitching a Dakota from Tengah heading for Butterworth, and in two hours the plane was touching down on the airfield with the island of Penang in the background, glistening like a pearl in the

Malacca Straits. I was intrigued to observe that the landing strip now ran from east to west, whilst in 1941 it was north to south. No explanation was offered as to why the Japs had changed direction, but I did notice that there were hundreds of Japanese prisoners, under the watchful gazes of armed Royal Engineers, busily toiling away constructing the runway as it was originally. Indeed, Japanese soldiers were being made to restore properties that had been desecrated.

I had an overwhelming desire, which I could not explain at the time, to cross the straits to Georgetown, on Penang Island. I knew in my heart that it would bring sadness. Nothing would be the same as it was when I was there in 1941, in peacetime conditions; and again in the house of the Wongs when Fruity, Brem and I were fugitives on the run. Yet I knew that I had to go to see for myself. A strange force within drove me on.

I hitched a ride on a RAF truck for the five miles to the ferry jetty. The straight road between tall trees was much the same as I remembered it. So too were the rather shabby dwellings of the small town of Butterworth. The old steam ferry had not changed either. As we chugged across the narrow strait I recalled the dark night at the end of 1941 when Brem, Fruity and I paddled silently, hardly daring to breathe, as we steered our borrowed sampan between the two shores. We could just make out the black menacing shapes of Japanese warships and a submarine. We were desperate then, behind Japanese lines, not knowing whether or not we would be taken into hiding at the house of Fruity's Chinese girlfriend Befung Wong.

The ferry tied up at the jetty, close to where we three young airmen, disguised as Chinese coolies, had run between the shafts of rickshaws containing our three Chinese girl friends, in order to get past the Jap sentries guarding the docks.

As the sun began to dip towards the horizon I trudged wearily, my heart leaden as I forced myself to think again about the present. On past the statue of Queen Victoria, which had somehow been spared by the Japs, up towards the main shopping centre of Georgetown. Many buildings had not been repaired since the bombings by American Flying Fortresses earlier in the year. Some of the shops were open for business, although goods for sale appeared sparse, as I sought out a small hotel that would serve me for a couple of nights or so.

I felt deeply depressed that night. Why was I here in Penang at all? Happy days on the island were in the past. The carefree times of four years ago, spent in the bars and dance halls, whilst some adjourned afterwards to the brothels, were all just memories now, as was the one fulfilled love of my life that began near here in the suburbs of the town. The future did not hold very much in prospect either. Back in England I would need to think seriously about earning a living. It would probably be several weeks before I would be demobilised. Perhaps I would stay on in the peacetime RAF? No. I had had enough of the life. Maybe if I had graduated to flight engineer I might have signed on for a few more years; but then I would still eventually have to face up to gaining a foothold in Civvy Street. By then it might not be so easy to make a fresh start. I dismissed out of hand thoughts of resuming my studies to become an accountant.

As I sat drinking at the bar I became more and more depressed. I thought about setting out to find a willing Chinese maiden; but dismissed the idea. I could not be bothered to engage myself in talking to a group of servicemen who were steadily becoming more and more rowdy in one corner of the saloon, so I staggered up to my room and passed out on the bed.

Chapter 20

The following morning my head had cleared, but my thoughts were not cheerful. Still I asked myself, why was I here? I knew that after breakfast I was going to set out to find the Wongs' villa, where the old sea captain, Wong Ten, would return to his family after each of his trading voyages. I knew that I would find no one there. I had seen his ship, the *Hang Tau*, sinking rapidly in the swirling waters of the Palembang River. My pilgrimage was doomed to lead to further sorrow.

As I stepped out into the street I was soon accosted by rickshaw coolies, plying for trade. Little did they know that the last time I had come that way I was actually pulling a rickshaw. They would not have believed me had I told them. 'Him wacky Englishman,' they would have thought.

Up past the police station I headed north towards the coastal road, the sea to my right, and beyond it the plains around Butterworth. In the distance, further to the north, in the sparkling light of the morning sun, I could just make out the hazy outline of Kedah Peak. It sent a shudder through my body as I thought back to that morning on 8 December 1941, at about the same time of the day, when a keen-sighted airman had begun running from the airfield towards the boundary trees, shouting and pointing towards the peak. There, just above it, I could just make out a large formation of aircraft heading straight towards us.

Still in a state of shock from the first raid soon after dawn, which had heralded dramatically the fact that we must be at war with Japan, I had scurried for the nearest slit trench, where the luck of the Gods was on my side. I had been living on borrowed time ever since.

We did not know then that eastwards across the international dateline the American Navy had just been smashed up at Pearl Harbour.

Now that the war was over there would be no formation of twenty-seven Mitsubishi bombers appearing over Kedah Peak. Still, I was leaden of heart as

114

I neared the Wong residence. I rounded a bend and there it was, from that distance looking much as I had remembered it, for it had been in my thoughts almost daily over the intervening years. There, on the seaward side, stood the little tower where the three Wong sisters had taken it in turns to gaze out to sea in search of their father's ship, while we three fugitive airmen remained below, out of sight of any possible informers for the Japanese.

I approached cautiously, but could see no sign of life. No one was around. I moved round to the rear of the building, to the door where Brem, Fruity and I had been smuggled in by Befung that fateful morning of New Year's Eve 1941.

To my surprise the door was slightly ajar. I crept warily inside. Clearly, the building had been occupied, probably by Japanese soldiers. The walls were filthy, rubbish was strewn around, and throughout was the stench of mildew and stale urine. Much of the furniture in the lounge was damaged. I moved towards the sleeping quarters and the room where cloth used to be stored that had been purchased from distant traders by Wong Ten. Strangely enough the area had been cleaned up and there were some bales of cloth piled up.

I crept slowly along the passageway towards the little room where Tau Fong and I had spent our first night together. I felt tears welling up and trickling gently down my cheeks as I thought about that first meeting, as I had done a thousand times over the years. For me the bliss of that very first fulfilment of sexual desire. I thought again of her warm lissome body next to mine. I turned away, unable to bear the sorrow any more.

Again there were signs that someone had been there not long since, for the room had been tidied up. For what reason, I wondered.

There was nothing to keep me here now, as I dragged my feet back towards the outside door. For some time I stood looking out from the doorway across the courtyard. I had reached the point of no return. Soon I would be heading back towards England and home.

In the distance I could just make out the figure of a Chinese maiden heading up the road. It has been said by Europeans that all Chinese look alike. To me that was not so. As she came nearer she began to look just like Tau Fong the last time I had seen her walking the deck of the good ship Hang Tau. I knew that I must be hallucinating. Perhaps it was simply my short sightedness that had ensured I would not be a pilot.

The girl came ever nearer as I stood there framed in the doorway. I could make out a puzzled look upon her face as she saw the Air Force uniform. Then the look changed to one of incredulity as she came nearer, and her eyes opened wide into that look I knew so well in surely what must be a previous life.

'Ken,' she gasped, 'surely it cannot be you?'

'You look like a girl I used to know; used to love very dearly,' I blurted out, 'but you must be a ghost.'

She dropped the basket she was carrying and ran the last few steps, reaching out to touch me, as if to see if I was real. I threw my arms around her, feeling the passion surging within my loins. 'Tau Fong, it cannot be you. I saw you swept away in that terrible river: but if it is not you what are you doing at this house?'

We were now held tightly in each other's arms as our lips met in a kiss that defied time.

We gazed long and deeply into each other's eyes. I let my hands run slowly down her shapely back. This was no ghost, but the lissome contours of the body I had carried in my mind and heart throughout this hideous war.

At last I broke the silence. 'How can you be here when I saw you swept away in those turgid brown waters, the same that claimed the stricken *Hang Tau*? As Brem and I struck out towards the Palembang Town shore we could see bodies and wreckage in the water, but no sign of you or your family.'

Sadness clouded Tau Fong's face as she replied, 'Yes, my father and elder brother were in the wheelhouse. They were killed instantly. My two sisters and Fruity were aft and were thrown into the water, probably injured. Koo and I never saw them again. We began to swim, but the current carried us downstream. Eventually we managed to reach the river bank some way down from Palembang, and on the other side of the river.' She paused. 'As you know, we had sailed from Penang hoping to join our relatives who had settled near to Palembang. We thought that the Japanese would not worry about occupying Sumatra, but of course, the oilfields were a prime target.'

'How did you cope with the occupation by the Japs?' I questioned.

'The Japs did not really bother us much. My uncle in Sumatra has a farm, mainly fruit, not far from where Koo and I landed, so he was able to make a living. We heard of atrocities committed by the soldiers in other places, but we were far enough out of town to be left in peace.'

'When did you return here?'

'Only one week ago. When the war finished I was able to fix a passage in a small ship sailing to Penang. I wanted to find out if my father's house here,

116

and the shop in town where I am staying, were still intact.' She cast her eyes downwards, with a look that I could not interpret.

'Why don't you come back inside?' she continued, 'I have some food in my basket, and I can make some tea. I was coming here to carry on clearing the mess that the soldiers left behind them.'

We went indoors, hand in hand, and she busied herself making tea and preparing a snack. While we ate and drank I told her what had happened to me since the fateful bombing of the *Hang Tau*. 'My time is up in this part of the world, and I am due to travel back to England very soon.'

When we had finished our repast Tau Fong rose from her kneeling position, holding out her hand to me. 'Come, and I will show you what clearing up I have done already.' She led me into the passageway. 'Do you remember this room?' she murmured.

'Of course I do, the memory has been locked in my heart for almost four years. You asked me to hand you my dirty shorts for washing. Then you undid your kimono, letting it fall to the floor. How could I forget it? I have not made love to anyone else since.'

'I can see that your shorts are not dirty now,' she murmured demurely. So saying she released her kimono, just as she had done before, revealing again the lissome body I had known so well.

I could not resist following her example; neither did she want me to, I was sure.

We sank on to the mattress entwined in the fulfilment of our passions. Our love for one another had not diminished.

Time went by without notice as I lay there in a daze. Opening my eyes again I saw that she was dressing. Seeing me looking at her she said, 'Stay here; I will be back in a while.' There was a solemnity in her voice that I did not understand.

When she moved out of my sight I began to dream about introducing her to my parents, and setting up home in England. To my mother all foreigners, especially those with a different coloured skin, were second class human beings; but I knew that she could not fail to be won over by the grace and charm of Tau Fong. Now in her sixties she had waited long to become a grandmother, and she must see that my dark haired maiden with the almond shaped eyes would bring many babies into the world.

After a while I dressed and moved to the doorway to await the return of Tau Fong.

It seemed an age, but probably not more than an hour had passed when I saw her in the distance again; but this time not alone. Beside her on one side was a slender dark haired youth probably in his early teens. Holding his hand was a fair-haired boy, who, when he drew nearer, looked about three years old. In Tau Fong's arms she appeared to be carrying a shawl.

As the little group came close to me I thought I could recognise the tall dark boy. Surely it was her younger brother Koo, who would have been around ten years old when last I saw him aboard the *Hang Tau*. But who was the little fair-haired boy, and the contents of the shawl, which I could now see concealed a baby. My emotions were in a turmoil, gripping me by the throat so that my tongue would not function.

Tau Fong was the first to speak, turning towards the tall dark lad. 'This is my brother Koo; you may remember him; he remembers you. And this little boy, who is now just three years old, is your son that I named Ken Wong.'

As the little lad looked up and smiled I was too amazed to speak. I just lifted him in the air and he began to chuckle.

'I have taught him some English,' said Tau Fong. 'He knows that his father was an airman, and what you looked like. I showed him a photograph of you taken in this very house. It was in my money pouch when the *Hang Tau* went down, and survived the wetting.'

Recovering my voice I could only blurt out, 'He is very beautiful, just like his mummy, but not a bit like his Dad, except for the fair hair. But who is the little baby?'

Tau Fong paused, casting her big luminous eyes downwards as she whispered almost inaudibly, 'He is mine too – and my husband's.'

It was my turn again to be struck dumb. All my dreams of the past hour were shattered in one sentence. I could not disguise my emotions as, in a cracked voice, I managed to reply, 'Congratulations on having such a lovely baby.'

Tau Fong was by now in tears, and the baby, sensing her sorrow, began to cry too.

Between sobs she whispered, 'His daddy is my second cousin. We fell in love in Sumatra and married. I did not think that I should ever see you again; but still I have your son whom I shall love for ever as I would have done you.'

We both wept in one another's embrace, the baby between us. I knew that I must leave now. There was nothing more to be said that would not hurt us more.

I turned slowly on my heels, dragging my feet towards the town, the ferry, and beyond that England. I did not dare even to turn around. Maybe, in time, I would meet someone I would love, but always a part of my heart would be in Malaya.